Is the BIBLE FACT or FICTION?

Is the BIBLE FACT or FICTION?

An Introduction to Biblical Historiography

Barbara E. Organ

BS635.3.O74 2004
Organ, Barbara E., 1942–
Is the Bible fact or
fiction? : an introduction
to biblical historiography
New York : Paulist Press,
c2004.

Paulist Press
New York/Mahwah, N.J.

Cover design by Sharyn Banks
Book design by Lynn Else

Library of Congress Cataloging-in-Publication Data

Organ, Barbara E., 1942–
    Is the Bible fact or fiction? : an introduction to biblical historiography / Barbara E. Organ.
        p.   cm.
    Includes bibliographical references.
    ISBN 0-8091-4236-8 (alk. paper)
    1. Bible—Historiography. I. Title.
BS635.3.O74 2004
220.6′7—dc22

                                                                2003021139

Published by Paulist Press
997 Macarthur Boulevard
Mahwah, New Jersey 07430

www.paulistpress.com

Printed and bound in the
United States of America

CONTENTS

1

INTRODUCTION:
HISTORY AND THE BIBLE

In the land of Israel today, tourism and archaeology are important sectors of the economy, and both are directly linked to avid interest in the Bible and its world. Tourists are often also pilgrims, eager to visit the sites of events described in the biblical texts, to walk on the same ground, to see the same vistas and feel the same air as the ancient prophets and kings, as Jesus and his disciples...to touch the same world they did. Here is where the foundational events of Judaism and Christianity took place, and visitors want to grasp their roots. Tourist guides faithfully retell the biblical accounts that lie behind each location; the very names on road signs stir the imagination in anticipation: Mount Carmel, Nazareth, Jericho, Bethlehem, and Jerusalem. Here is where it all happened.

Or did it? Archaeology in the last generation has raised some serious doubts about the when and the where of biblical events: Jericho was not standing at the supposed time of its conquest (Josh 2–4); in fact, there was no conquest! Israel consisted of local tribes amalgamated under the banner of their god Yahweh. For most scholars, the patriarchs are not to be seen as historical figures; even Moses and the exodus have come under strict scrutiny, with the result of a severe downsizing of the exodus event—if it occurred at all. More recently, David, Solomon, and much of the monarchy have come under fire. Where is the archaeological evidence? Where is the historical evidence? What happened to the history in the biblical books? If it did not happen as written, what now? Is this all fiction?

A recent article in a popular archaeological magazine reviewed the same issues. In an article entitled "Scholars Talk about How the

Field Has Changed," the editor remarked that "the last 25 years have witnessed a sea change in almost everything connected with Biblical archaeology." The scholars interviewed had less confidence in the historicity of the Bible, but also pointed out that archaeology and the biblical texts provide two different kinds of information and must be analyzed separately.[1]

Is there any history in the Bible? The short answer is yes. The longer answer is, it depends on what you mean by history. What *is* history? It may come as a surprise that we even have to ask the question. Surely history is simply what happened in a past time. That is certainly the starting point, but there is obviously more. Do we want to know how ordinary people lived, their housing, diet, clothing, marriage customs, and so forth, or do we want to know political history—who the rulers were; how they dealt with other nations; what treaties, wars, and power struggles they were involved in? The initial question will dictate the kind of research undertaken by the historian. Ultimately, we may want to know it all, but the research has to be focused on one question at a time. For example, does the historian want to write a narrow history of a particular city for a short period of time, or does the historian want to sketch a far-ranging view of international events over several centuries? The purpose of a history will determine its content: political or social, local or international, narrowly focused or with a broad perspective.

Beyond that, there is also the issue of point of view. Although modern historians especially try to take an objective stand, each historian has her or his own perspective and opinion on the unfolding of a history. The years of and after the Protestant Reformation can be told from a Protestant or a Catholic perspective; what might be stressed in one could be glossed over in the other. No two people, let alone historians, see events from the same standpoint. Even unconsciously, the historian's bias (not necessarily a negative thing) comes through.

---

1. *Biblical Archaeology Review* 27/7 (March/April 2001), 22–25, 29–31, 35. This magazine, directed to a general readership, contains up-to-date articles by recognized biblical scholars and archaeologists. It is also well illustrated with outstanding photography.

So the question is not only what *is* history, but whose history is it? More recently it has been pointed out that histories are written by the winners. That is, the people who are commissioned to record and retell events have often been employed by those who are in power politically, economically, or socially. This does not mean that their version of events is wrong, only that there is a greater chance that other points of view will not be well represented, if at all. For example, political history—the history of leaders and nations and wars—has been the norm rather than the history of the "little people"—the everyday lives of the unknown many. Women, too, have largely been left out of history books until fairly recently.

Fundamentally, history is about what happened in a time gone by. The problem is, how does the historian know what happened in a time gone by? Historians rely on written records—official documents, treaties, letters, military dispatches and maps, diaries and memoirs, tax records, household accounts…the list goes on. Anything and everything that can elucidate what happened is grist to the historian's mill. They study the places where events occurred to understand how the incidents recorded fit into the geography of the land or to assess the accuracy of the written record. Clearly the more literate the society, the more documentation will be produced, and the more recent the events, the likelier the chances of that documentation's survival, not to mention the greater the chances of being able to verify the data. Understandably, documentation from the ancient world is sparse and is often fragmentary where it does exist.

Historiography

We think of historians as recording facts—and so they do, but they also do much more. The facts of what happened would be little more than a list of incidents with relevant names and dates, a form of record known as annals. Historians go beyond the mere recital of facts to a deeper comprehension of events, to analysis of causes, effects, and complications, and to assessment. Historians may assess the accuracy of earlier records or the impact of certain

3

events or comment on the judgment of the major participants (just consider the various assessments of any former U.S. president). Here is where their own system of values comes into play, whether a political leaning to left or right, or a critical stance towards patriarchy, or a view of the world from a Western perspective or Third-World perspective, and so forth. This is what historiography—the writing of a history—entails.

Historians choose what to write about. They decide the period, the range of material, the level of detail, what to include, and what to exclude. This is only reasonable: It is not possible to include every single incident, name, and item of interest. But the issue remains that historians make choices, and the reader needs to remember that fact. There may be more information, there may be another point of view. While this is true of modern historians who have colleagues to challenge and disagree if necessary, it is no less true of ancient historians, whose critics (if any) we know nothing about. We therefore must analyze their history writing bearing in mind the lack of another voice to balance or complement what we learn.

After collecting and analyzing the evidence available, historians reconstruct a history, a version of what happened. They narrate a coherent "story" of what happened, what were the contributing factors, what were the repercussions, what changes resulted in this set of events. A history, then, is a narrative with a starting point and a concluding point. As a narrative it is also a literary work and conforms to accepted literary style. Historians include "characters" whose motives can be probed, surmised from their actions, and assessed according to some standard—of military expertise, or stable government, or virtue, or principle, and so forth. It is possible, then, to discover the historian's perspective and use of materials and characters in the overall narrative. It is also possible to evaluate whether the historian has produced a reliable reconstruction of what happened or whether the history has been shaped more by ideology than by actual events.

The same is true of ancient history writing, perhaps more so. Ancient historians had fewer resources available to them and more freedom in narrating. Their guiding principle was not simply the reconstruction of events but the reconstruction of events in such a way as to edify, to teach a lesson for life, to make a moral point—and to do this artistically. If the historian wished to demonstrate a pattern in history, it was permissible to rearrange events or chronology to do so. No modern historian could get away with that today. The motives of a character in the history could be presented through a speech, composed for that purpose. Events could be dramatized to create interest. All this would bring shivers to a modern history department.

The purpose of this book is to look at some aspects of the biblical historical books, not so much to identify what actually happened as to identify the kind of historiography the writers undertook. How did the biblical authors write their histories, and what sort of history did they think they were writing? Several elements must be considered: How was history perceived in the ancient world? What was the aim of each author? What resources did each author have? How much license did ancient historians have in their compositions? And what role did literary style play? Even considering such questions alerts us to the limitations of ancient history writing and to our re-reading of it. Then, too, we moderns are at a great distance of time, not to mention culture and language, from the biblical writers and need to take that factor into account.

This is where archaeology comes into the picture. The further into the past the historian ventures, the less documentation, and thus the less evidence, is available. Archaeology provides evidence not only in the form of more documentation discovered (clay tablets, scrolls, inscriptions) and everyday artifacts (pottery, tools, weapons) but also in recovering buildings, fortifications, streets, and even locales of forgotten towns and villages—all of which go towards reconstructing a society and the form it took. Archaeology may not be able to provide exactly the kind of evidence the historian would like—information about particular individuals, for example—but can indicate whether the traditions are accurate regarding place locations, topography of a remembered battle, or even general social conditions. Problems arise, naturally, when archaeological evidence contradicts or calls into question in some way the received traditions of a particular group of people. That is the case with many of the received traditions of the biblical text.

Literary studies, too, have shed light on the historical biblical books—indeed on all biblical texts. The Bible may be sacred literature but it is first of all literature, and that aspect must also be taken into consideration. The definition of genre, or type, of writing is crucial. Clearly, we would not read poetry in the same way as a legal document, nor would we view a newspaper cartoon in the same way as a news photo. To confuse the genre is to confuse the purpose of a text and ultimately to miss its meaning. Among the biblical books, should we read Paul's letters in the same way as the Book of Genesis? It seems obvious that we are dealing with two very different kinds of writing, which must be understood each in its own context. The more difficult question is, should we read Paul's letters in the same way as the Book of Acts? How different are these two kinds of writing? At the very least, we must take into account that they were written by two distinct individuals, separated by a generation or so, writing for separate purposes. All this affects the way we understand their writings.

The biblical histories are not all cut from the same cloth; each has its own pattern and style, not to mention purpose. Once we realize that all books are not alike, we are well on the way to discovering the creativity and theology of each author, not to mention the varied richness and depth of the Bible as a whole. It does mean that we can no longer afford to read the Bible simply at the surface level, but the extra attention paid to literary concerns will be abundantly rewarded.

Fact or Fiction?

That having been said, it is true that analysis of the historical books in the Bible raises questions about the "facts" just as archaeology does, although in another fashion. If this is so, if the biblical tradition is contradicted or at least not supported by the findings of modern research, what can be said about these books? Are they pious fictions? Or are they a form of historiography? Our purpose in the following chapters is to explore this question. Until fairly recently, the history as presented in the Bible was taken for granted. Modern books on the history of Israel or of Christianity followed the biblical accounts faithfully. But as we have seen, recent scholarship has taught us to be cautious about assuming that "what really happened" is just as the biblical books describe. Further, since these accounts often act as models for ongoing attitudes and action, the issue of how to understand such historical accounts has repercussions beyond the pages of the Bible or simple curiosity. Was it really divine will to "destroy utterly" the inhabitants of Canaan when the Israelites settled there? How unified was the Christian Church in its early days?

The modern historian wants factual evidence, some sort of record of an event. The records may vary in value from a passing reference in someone's correspondence to a defeated politician's memoirs to official government archives. In the case of the ancient world, the modern historian has to make do with far less and much different kinds of materials: inscriptions (partial or complete); pieces of archival material, such as lists of kings or cities; battle accounts (usually by the victors); and, above all, stories. Historians have to sift through stories for historical kernels, weighing what they glean against probability, against archaeological remains, even against other stories. Reconstructing the history of the ancient world is fraught with difficulties.

The ancient historians also wanted evidence and were not unsophisticated about evaluating their sources, which would have looked very like the sources used by modern historians: archival records, lists, copies of treaties and letters, and stories of political and religious leaders, as well as their own observations on the contemporaneous situation. There are, of course, differences, largely in the treatment of material. The historians of old had access to a far narrower range of materials than their modern counterparts, and they also had a clear intent to teach a moral lesson and to entertain, to make their histories interesting—so that people would read them! The aesthetics of history writing was an important component. The ancient historians had more freedom in rearranging material—even chronology—in order to make a point. They also had greater license in the reconstruction of events, including dramatizations of events and speeches of which there could be no factual record. Speeches especially were composed to reveal the motivation of characters in the history. Ancient historiography, then, was shaped by several considerations, and not least by the writer's ideology—the philosophy or theology that they intended to promote. They were not impartial observers but sometimes passionate advocates.

The Historical Books

With all this in mind we shall approach the biblical texts to discover what they can tell us about the way biblical authors wrote. The purpose is not so much to discover "what really happened" in order to reconstruct an accurate history—that is far more complex than can be undertaken here. Instead, we hope to uncover the style and purpose of the biblical authors to determine, as far as possible, their ideologies, and so finally to know how to interpret their writings. In each case texts are provided but further reading of the biblical context is strongly recommended.

At this point we should identify the books we refer to as "historical." In the Old Testament, several books have been thought of (at least in the past) as actual histories: Joshua and Judges, the books of Samuel and Kings, Chronicles, and Ezra-Nehemiah. These are included in the Former Prophets of the Hebrew Bible. Catholic Bibles, however, following the ancient Greek translation known as the Septuagint, also include 1 and 2 Maccabees as "historical" books; they are not to be found in the Hebrew Bible, nor in the Protestant Bible. Christians in the New Testament also have the Acts of the Apostles, which deals with the history of the early church.

In the current book we move backwards through the Bible and through time. The first section will treat the early Christian community, whose narrative is told in the Acts of the Apostles, a second section will deal with a volatile period of Jewish history, related in the books of the Maccabees, and the last section will turn to the broad-ranging history of Israel narrated in Joshua through 2 Kings.

For Further Reading

Two helpful and interesting publications are the *Biblical Archaeology Review*, published by the Biblical Archaeology Society, Washington, D.C., and *The Bible Today*, published by the Liturgical Press, Collegeville, MN.

William G. Dever, *What Did the Biblical Writers Know and When Did They Know It?* (Grand Rapids, MI: Eerdmans, 2001)

"David's Jerusalem: Fiction or Reality?"—a set of three articles with differing conclusions in *Biblical Archaeology Review*, 26/2 (March/April 2000).

For Further Study

Read Judges 14, 1 Kings 4, and Acts 4:32–5:11. Consider the kind and value of historical sources used in these chapters. What kind of language is used? Is it prosaic or imaginative, storytelling or businesslike? What elements could not have been verified by an impartial observer?

2

DIFFERENCES OF OPINION:
ONE CONFERENCE, TWO REPORTS

This first section will explore aspects of the Book of Acts, the biblical book that looks most like history to the modern eye and that has been widely accepted as a reliable account of the early church. This narrative of the early days of Christianity has consequently provided the outline for many a modern history of the church. Yet there are difficulties that lead us to question what kind of history we are dealing with. As a way of entering into the historiography of Acts, we shall focus on incidents involving Paul, the early Christian missionary, and then reflect on how the author of Acts has reconstructed the history of first generation Christians. This chapter and the next will look at issues and events related in both Paul's letters and Acts, while Chapters 4 and 5 will examine Paul's conversion, narrated only in Acts.

A First Reading

From the strictly historical standpoint, an overview of Christian origins looks something like this: Sometime around the year 28 C.E.,[1] a young preacher appeared on the scene in Galilee, a region of the Roman province of Syria. Hailed by the people as a prophet and wonder-worker, the young preacher, Jesus of Nazareth, made his way to Jerusalem, which was the religious center of his people, the Jews. There he fell afoul of the authorities and was executed by the Roman

---

1. C.E. (Common Era) and B.C.E. (Before the Common Era) are designations preferred by many scholars instead of A.D. (*Anno Domini*) and B.C. (Before Christ).

governor, probably in 30 C.E., but his followers claimed that he was still alive, resurrected from the dead, and they began to preach in his name in Jerusalem and elsewhere. These followers claimed he was their messiah, a figure greatly anticipated in some circles of Judaism. The beginning and spread of the movement is hazy but they experienced such success in attracting followers, especially among non-Jews, or Gentiles, that their communities were soon found all over the Roman Empire. As they spread in the Greek-speaking parts of the empire, they came to be known as Christians, from the Greek term for *messiah,* which is *christos.* As Christians, this group became separated from their Jewish origins and grew into a considerable community, or church, so that by the end of the fourth century Christianity actually became the official religion of the Roman Empire.

Interest in the origins and early development of this community is not dampened by the lack of information; on the contrary, scholars pore over every available bit of evidence to try to reconstruct whatever they can of Christianity in the first century. One of their resources is the Christian (New) Testament, especially the book known as the Acts of the Apostles. We can join this enterprise in a small way by examining the way Acts narrates events in the life of the first Christian community. Here we shall explore two accounts of a meeting between Paul and the Christian leaders of Jerusalem, about 48 or 49 C.E., one taken from Acts (15:1–35) and the other from Paul's own version of events (Gal 2:1–10). By comparing the two accounts, we shall begin to see how Acts as history reconstructs its own understanding of the early church's growth.

Acts 15:6–35

6. The apostles and the elders met together to consider this matter. 7. After there had been much debate, Peter stood up and said to them, "My brothers, you know that in the early days God made a choice among you, that I should be the one through whom the Gentiles would hear the message of the good news and become believers. 8. And God,

who knows the human heart, testified to them by giving them the Holy Spirit, just as he did to us; 9. and in cleansing their hearts by faith he has made no distinction between them and us. 10. Now therefore why are you putting God to the test by placing on the neck of the disciples a yoke that neither our ancestors nor we have been able to bear? 11. On the contrary, we believe that we will be saved through the grace of the Lord Jesus, just as they will."

12. The whole assembly kept silence, and listened to Barnabas and Paul as they told of all the signs and wonders that God had done through them among the Gentiles. 13. After they finished speaking, James replied, "My brothers, listen to me. 14. Simeon has related how God first looked favorably on the Gentiles, to take from among them a people for his name. 15. This agrees with the words of the prophets, as it is written, 16. 'After this I will return, and I will rebuild the dwelling of David, which has fallen; from its ruins I will rebuild it, and I will set it up, 17. so that all other peoples may seek the Lord—even all the Gentiles over whom my name has been called. Thus says the Lord, who has been making these things 18. known from long ago.' 19. Therefore I have reached the decision that we should not trouble those Gentiles who are turning to God, 20. but we should write to them to abstain only from things polluted by idols and from fornication and from whatever has been strangled and from blood. 21. For in every city, for generations past, Moses has had those who proclaim him, for he has been read aloud every sabbath in the synagogues."

22. Then the apostles and the elders, with the consent of the whole church, decided to choose men from among their members and to send them to Antioch with Paul and Barnabas. They sent Judas called Barsabbas, and Silas, leaders among the brothers, 23. with the following letter: "The brothers, both the apostles and the elders, to the

believers of Gentile origin in Antioch and Syria and Cilicia, greetings. 24. Since we have heard that certain persons who have gone out from us, though with no instructions from us, have said things to disturb you and have unsettled your minds, 25. we have decided unanimously to choose representatives and send them to you, along with our beloved Barnabas and Paul, 26. who have risked their lives for the sake of our Lord Jesus Christ. 27. We have therefore sent Judas and Silas, who themselves will tell you the same things by word of mouth. 28. For it has seemed good to the Holy Spirit and to us to impose on you no further burden than these essentials: 29. that you abstain from what has been sacrificed to idols and from blood and from what is strangled and from fornication. If you keep yourselves from these, you will do well. Farewell."

30. So they were sent off and went down to Antioch. When they gathered the congregation together, they delivered the letter. 31. When its members read it, they rejoiced at the exhortation. 32. Judas and Silas, who were themselves prophets, said much to encourage and strengthen the believers. 33. After they had been there for some time, they were sent off in peace by the believers to those who had sent them.[2] 35. But Paul and Barnabas remained in Antioch, and there, with many others, they taught and proclaimed the word of the Lord.

In a first reading, the account seems quite straightforward. Some believers, perhaps associated with the Pharisee movement (v. 5), appeared in Antioch (see 14:26–28), teaching that the Jewish tradition of circumcision must be maintained for salvation. Since Paul and Barnabas disagreed with this tradition, they were sent to Jerusalem to discuss the issue with the apostles. After a debate, during which Peter argues that the Gentiles not be required to bear this

---

2. NRSV omits v. 34, "But it seemed good to Silas to remain there," not found in all manuscripts.

burden, James[3] expressed the decision that nothing should be asked of Gentiles except to refrain from "things polluted by idols and from fornication and from whatever has been strangled and from blood." Paul and Barnabas were sent back to Antioch with a letter announcing this decision. We turn now to Paul's letter to the Galatians.

Gal 2:1–15

1. Then after fourteen years I went up again to Jerusalem with Barnabas, taking Titus along with me. 2. I went up in response to a revelation. Then I laid before them (though only in a private meeting with the acknowledged leaders) the gospel that I proclaim among the Gentiles, in order to make sure that I was not running, or had not run, in vain. 3. But even Titus, who was with me, was not compelled to be circumcised, though he was a Greek. 4. But because of false believers secretly brought in, who slipped in to spy on the freedom we have in Christ Jesus, so that they might enslave us—5. we did not submit to them even for a moment, so that the truth of the gospel might always remain with you. 6. And from those who were supposed to be acknowledged leaders (what they actually were makes no difference to me; God shows no partiality)—those leaders contributed nothing to me. 7. On the contrary, when they saw that I had been entrusted with the gospel for the uncircumcised, just as Peter had been entrusted with the gospel for the circumcised 8. (for he who worked through Peter making him an apostle to the circumcised also worked through me in sending me to the Gentiles), 9. and when James and Cephas and John, who were acknowledged pillars, recognized the grace that had been given to me, they gave to Barnabas and me the right hand of fellowship, agreeing that we should go to

---

3. This is not the James—the son of Zebedee and brother of John, one of the Twelve—who was executed by Herod Agrippa (Acts 12:2), but James the brother of the Lord (Gal 1:19), who was the leader of the Jerusalem church.

the Gentiles and they to the circumcised. 10. They asked only one thing, that we remember the poor, which was actually what I was eager to do.

11. But when Cephas came to Antioch, I opposed him to his face, because he stood self-condemned; 12. for until certain people came from James, he used to eat with the Gentiles. But after they came, he drew back and kept himself separate for fear of the circumcision faction. 13. And the other Jews joined him in this hypocrisy, so that even Barnabas was led astray by their hypocrisy. 14. But when I saw that they were not acting consistently with the truth of the gospel, I said to Cephas before them all, "If you, though a Jew, live like a Gentile and not like a Jew, how can you compel the Gentiles to live like Jews?" 15. We ourselves are Jews by birth and not Gentile sinners;

Here we have Paul's own account of what seems to be the same event: a journey from Antioch to meet with the Jerusalem leaders. The issue to be discussed is not entirely clear from this excerpt, but on closer examination turns out to be the question of circumcision (v. 3; see also 5:2). James, the Lord's brother, and Peter (Paul regularly calls him Cephas, the Aramaic version of his name) agreed that what Paul was doing—preaching the gospel to the uncircumcised—was acceptable. Sometime afterward, Peter went to Antioch, where he freely ate with Gentiles, but later refrained from so doing on the arrival of the "circumcision faction." Paul says he criticized Peter to his face for his hypocrisy.

The two passages in Acts and Galatians are in agreement over the following points: (a) a delegation from Antioch went to Jerusalem; (b) there was a debate over the issue of circumcision for Gentiles; (c) the issue is a serious and possibly divisive one; (d) Paul was accompanied by Barnabas; (e) James and Peter (Cephas) were among the Jerusalem leaders; and (f) the two sides agreed there should be no circumcision for Gentiles. There are, however, some major and minor discrepancies that are worth exploring.

A Second Reading

At this point we read the two passages again, more closely this time, taking note of the differences between the two accounts. Three questions arise quite quickly: What was the nature of the meeting—public or private? Who took the lead in welcoming Gentiles into the community? And what was the debate about—circumcision or Torah observance?

First, what was the nature of the meeting—was it public or private? Paul's account seems to refer to a private meeting that had been undertaken on his initiative (Gal 1:2), whereas in Acts Paul and Barnabas had been delegated by the Antioch church to approach the Jerusalem church: "Paul and Barnabas and some of the others were appointed to go" (15:2). Paul also emphasizes his equal standing with the Jerusalem leadership, even to the point of downplaying their importance ("supposed to be acknowledged leaders" who "contributed nothing to me," Gal 2:6). Elsewhere, Paul parallels himself with the other apostles (1 Cor 9:1–5) in a way that suggests he is somewhat sensitive about his position. Nonetheless, he apparently found it advisable to check with the Jerusalem leaders about the way he preaches the gospel (Gal 2:2). He admits that they had no objections to his mission and parted from him on terms of friendship and fellowship. Paul also says that Titus accompanied him and Barnabas to Jerusalem. The presence of Titus might not have been very significant but for the statement that Titus, a Greek (that is, a Gentile), was not required to be circumcised, a fact that supports Paul's position. That having been said, however, it is noteworthy that Paul did find it necessary to consult with the Jerusalem leadership, in spite of his avowed independence. And the presence of Barnabas, possibly the senior of the two,[4] suggests that Paul accompanied him rather than the other way around. This could point to a more formal delegation from Antioch, as Acts claims.

In Acts, however, we have two churches dealing with an issue of concern to all. Whereas Paul's description is of a private meeting

---

4. According to Acts, Barnabas appears as Paul's mentor (Acts 9:27; 11:25).

with the "pillars" of the Jerusalem church, Acts refers to some kind of assembly, with an intervention by Peter, followed by the witness of Barnabas and Paul, all of which seems to lead to the decision of James. Note that it is James, the leader of the Jerusalem church, who makes the final decision (v. 19), rather than Peter or another of the apostles. The agreement of apostles and elders, with the entire community, indicates their involvement in the decision. This is confirmed in the letter, which says "it has seemed good to the Holy Spirit *and to us*" (v. 28).[5] The letter is to go not only to Antioch, where the issue was raised in the first place, but to all of Syria and Cilicia, a much wider audience than expected. This is now a community decision involving more than the local community. The decision, furthermore, seems to be about something more than circumcision, a question to which we shall turn later.[6]

Another, perhaps less obvious, difference is the matter of who took the lead in welcoming Gentiles into the believing community. According to Acts, there is a debate among the apostles and elders during which Peter makes a speech with a surprising claim. He says that God chose him to be the one through whom the Gentiles would hear the gospel message. Further, he makes a plea that Gentiles not be subject to the same "yoke that neither our ancestors nor we have been able to bear" (v. 10). Peter makes the point that God makes no distinction between Gentile and Jewish believers. Here, Peter is alluding also to an earlier incident related in Acts 10–11, an encounter with a Gentile believer heralded in a dream of clean and unclean animals. Those Gentiles received the Holy Spirit although they had not been circumcised, which created a precedent for the current debate in Jerusalem. Moreover, the encounter with the Gentiles involved eating with them, for which Peter was criticized on his return to Jerusalem (11:2–3). Peter had then pointed to his dream as justification for his

---

5. Italics here and in later scripture quotations are all added for emphasis.

6. The meeting related in Acts is also known as the "Council of Jerusalem" and the decision, with its accompanying letter, as the "Apostolic Decree." Both terms are avoided here because they raise other historical questions. See Commentaries and Bible Dictionaries.

actions, which the outpouring of the Spirit confirmed. Peter, according to Acts, is the one through whom the mission to the Gentiles gets its initiative and authorization.

Paul would certainly not agree. In the letter to the Galatians he claims that his mission to the Gentiles derives directly from God (1:11–12), without consultation with anyone else (1:16–17). It is the uniqueness of Paul's mission that eventually (after fourteen years!) sent him to Jerusalem to be validated by the leaders. In this letter, Paul says that the leaders recognized that he "had been entrusted with the gospel to the uncircumcised, just as Peter had been entrusted with the gospel for the circumcised" (2:7), and he reports that they agreed to continue on their different paths (2:9).

Further, the actions of Peter in withdrawing from table fellowship occurred *after* the meeting in Jerusalem, which seems odd if Paul and Acts are referring to the same event. That would mean that Peter, having just claimed the initiative in bringing Gentiles into the community and claiming for them a more flexible approach to Torah observance, now is unable to eat with non-observant Gentile Christians. Had Peter entirely forgotten his speech, not to mention his defense of his actions earlier at Joppa (Acts 11)?

Finally, was the debate about circumcision or Torah observance? So far the debate has been about the necessity of circumcision for Gentile converts, but the decision made by James and the Jerusalem church does not refer to this. Rather, James's speech concerns the extent of Torah observance for Jews:[7]

> Therefore I have reached the decision that we should not trouble those Gentiles who are turning to God, but we should write to them to abstain only from things polluted by idols and from fornication and from whatever has been strangled and from blood. (vv. 19–20)

---

7. Jewish tradition follows certain observances, including purification and dietary requirements of the Torah (or the Law of Moses, a term referring both to the first five books of the Bible and to the legal tradition deriving from them).

A word of explanation is in order here. The "things polluted by idols" ("what has been sacrificed to idols" in the letter) refers to foods offered in sacrifice in the Greek and Roman temples. Trade and professional organizations held their regular festivals by offering sacrifice to their patron deity and consuming the meat of the sacrifice in a banquet. Eating such meat could imply acknowledgment of the deity and approval of polytheistic ritual, intolerable to Jews.[8] The prohibitions against "whatever has been strangled" and "blood" refer to Jewish requirements for properly slaughtered animals. "Fornication" here probably refers to marriage within prohibited degrees of marriage. All of these prohibitions derive from the Holiness code of Leviticus 17–18, and are applied not only to the people of Israel but also to resident aliens, that is, Gentiles.

James's decision, then, concerns Torah observance for Gentiles, and represents a compromise position, waiving everything except these restrictions from the Law. Notice that James remarks that those who attend the synagogue are acquainted with "Moses," that is, with the Torah readings. The followers of Jesus as Messiah (Christ) have not yet separated from Judaism; they are Jews debating whether or not Gentile converts need to be fully observant. In the present passage, however, while there is no specific response to the question of circumcision, Peter's speech and the general context imply that the Gentiles are exempt from that Torah requirement.

Paul, on the other hand, in his own account makes no reference to any letter or indeed to any stipulations that Gentiles must accept. In other words, it appears Paul does not know about any such decision or letter. According to him, the Jerusalem leaders agreed to let Paul continue with his mission to the Gentiles, while they would continue theirs to the circumcised, with only one other request, to remember the poor. If there had been an agreement over food restrictions, there would have been no trouble in Antioch over Peter's table fellowship: Gentiles would have already been observing

---

8. Paul deals with this question in 1 Cor 8; it was obviously a contentious issue.

the food restrictions and Peter would not have had to withdraw when the more observant believers arrived.

Having compared the two accounts and discovered some differences, we return (again!) to those same accounts to read each on its own terms.

Acts 15:1–35 Revisited

One theme that emerges in this passage is that of leadership. Note the references to apostles and elders (vv. 2, 4, 6, 22, 23). Note which individuals actually speak in the assembly: Peter and James. Both, in fact, have suitably long speeches. Another theme is the community of believers: In this regard, note "they were sent on their way by the church" (v. 3), "welcomed by the church" (v. 4), "the whole church" (v. 22), "the assembly/congregation" (vv. 12, 30).[9] The word *brothers* (vv. 1, 23, 33) seems also to function as a synonym for assembly or church. Finally, there is the emphasis on unity: sending a delegation to Jerusalem for consultation, being welcomed by the churches, the consent of the whole church being given to the decision, the positive reception of the letter.

In Acts, we see a community problem resolved by community discussion. One church has sent a delegation to seek a solution at the mother church in Jerusalem, where the apostles can be found, who clearly have a pre-eminent position, and elders. Besides the witness of Paul and Barnabas, there are speeches by Peter, known as chief of the apostles, and James of Jerusalem, the brother of the Lord. There can be no more definitive or authoritative voices. The decision is ratified by the whole church and is forwarded by letter carried by designated messenger not only to Antioch but further afield, to Syria and Cilicia. While the Gentiles are to be left unburdened by circumcision, there are some requirements from the Mosaic law. Here is a portrait of a church with apostolic leadership, with lines of commu-

---

9. In Greek, the same word: *to pléthos*.

nication and authority, that can resolve a difficult issue in harmony; in other words, this is a well-organized church.

Gal 2:1–10 Revisited

Paul, on the other hand, presents us with a different portrait. He speaks of pursuing his own mission without consultation. This is especially clear in Gal 1:11–12, 15–19, but the idea continues in our passage: "I went up in response to a revelation." Notice the language: "I went up," "I laid before them," "the gospel that I proclaim," etc. He goes to confer with the "supposed" leaders only, not as a subordinate to superiors but as an equal among equals; again, his language insists on his independent status (vv. 5–6), and claims the leaders acknowledged his status, rather than the other way around (vv. 7–9). Paul even insists that this was a private meeting (v. 2).

The picture Paul presents of the believers is in contrast to that of Acts. Paul addresses a divided, if not confused, community in Galatia following another teaching or interpretation of the gospel message (1:6–9); in Antioch, Paul had to deal with "false believers," who came in "secretly," to "spy" and "enslave" (2:4)—all harsh words. He speaks of Peter's "fear" and "hypocrisy," and says that he challenged Peter to his face (2:11–14). This Peter is not the initiator of a mission to the Gentiles, who declares that table fellowship is acceptable; on the contrary, Peter aligns himself with the "circumcision faction" (v. 12). Nor does Peter look like a leader here. James, too, seems to be allied with this "circumcision faction"; in fact, it looks as if he sent this delegation, and thus suggests that James belongs to the more observant group.

What is to be made of these two accounts, more different than at first appears? It has been suggested that these two versions concern two different events, one a private meeting between Paul and the Jerusalem leadership and the other an assembly in Jerusalem to discuss the same issue of circumcision and Gentile observance. Most scholars, however, hold that Acts 15 and Gal 2:1–10 are parallel references to the same meeting. The answer lies in the nature of Acts and Galatians, that is, in their respective genre or literary type, and in their different points of view. Each deals with the situation in a different context. To this question we turn in the next chapter.

For Further Reading

R. E. Brown and John Meier, *Antioch and Rome: New Testament Cradles of Catholic Christianity* (Mahwah, NJ: Paulist Press, 1983), Chapter 2, "The Antiochene Church of the First Christian Generation."

Schuyler Brown, *The Origins of Christianity: A Historical Introduction to the New Testament* (Oxford/New York: Oxford University Press, 1984), Chapter 5, "Neither Jew nor Greek."

Frederick. J. Cwiekowski, *The Beginnings of Christianity* (Mahwah, NJ: Paulist Press, 1988), Chapter 4, "The First Christian Communities."

André Lemaire, "Burial Box of James the Brother of Jesus," *Biblical Archaeology Review* (November/December 2002), 24–33.

Hershel Shanks, ed., *Christianity and Rabbinic Judaism: A Parallel History of Their Origins and Early Development* (Washington, D.C.: Biblical Archaeology Society, 1992).

Stephen G. Wilson, *Related Strangers: Jews and Christians 70–170 C.E.* (Minneapolis: Fortress Press, 1995).

For Further Study

1. Read the story of the conversion of Cornelius in Acts 10:1–11:18. What is the role of the speeches in this narrative?

2. For historical context, find out more about eating meals in Greek and Roman temples. Read 1 Cor 8:1–13 and 10:14–32. What is Paul's position on eating meat associated with sacrifice?

3

DIFFERENT PURPOSES:
GALATIANS AND ACTS IN CONTEXT

Our ultimate goal is to understand how Acts is written, and in order to do this we must evaluate its version of events. In the present case we can assess the relative merits of Acts 15 against the account in Galatians. If we start with this letter, we can make the following observations. Paul is relating a first-person account of a personal experience, and he is closer in time to the events being remembered, and writing, moreover, to people who knew something of the issues. The letter to the Galatians was written somewhere about 54 C.E., only a few years after the meeting in Jerusalem, which most scholars estimate occurred around 48 or 49 C.E. Acts, on the other hand, was probably written somewhere around 80–85 C.E., fifty or more years after the events concerning Jesus of Nazareth and the beginning of the Christian community. Distance in time can be advantageous in bringing the larger picture into focus, but it can be disadvantageous in being removed from the actual events and perhaps from the people who could provide insight and correction. In this case, Paul's version is generally conceded as being more reliable; that is, his version of events is taken as being closer to the historical situation, although it is acknowledged that there are problems, particularly with Paul's bias.

The fact that we are dealing with a letter also has to be taken into consideration. A letter is by its nature one-sided. It is clear that Paul is writing in response to some situation that he does not specify but presumably the recipients are well aware of it. We, however, have to deduce what was happening in the Galatian church from Paul's reaction, which is clearly negative. Paul in his letter is not writing history, but putting forward arguments to affirm his stand that circumcision is not necessary for the Gentile believers. Because it is a letter, we have to make allowances for Paul's emphasis on his own role, which Paul may possibly have overstated, and for his strong language (for example, 1:6; 2:4; 3:1). Paul's use of strong, negative language about his opponents is consistent with the rhetoric of the day; in fact, his language gets even stronger as the letter proceeds so that he claims circumcision is in fact a hindrance, a denial even, of Christ's salvation (5:2–12). Here we get a glimpse of the man, his impatience (1:6, 8, 9; 3:1), his sarcasm (5:12), his assertiveness (2:11, 14). On the other hand, he also tries to be precise in his recitation of facts (see, for example, Gal 1:18–20 and 1 Cor 1:14–16). These characteristics add to the liveliness of the letter, making Paul seem closer to us and very real. At the same time, however, recognizing his bold style and his polemical stand will make any measured assessment of his judgments more necessary.

All that having been said, there is no reason to disbelieve the basic outline of Paul's version of events, even if it is prudent to tone down his self-assessment. Paul certainly understood himself as the apostle to the Gentiles, on a par with the other apostles (1 Cor 9: 1–2), with a radical approach (1 Cor 9:19–23). His letters resound with his insistence that Christ has freed believers from the law; in this he is consistent.

According to Paul, then, he and Barnabas went from the church at Antioch to Jerusalem to confer with the leadership there over the necessity of circumcision for Gentiles. They received a favorable hearing, with no restrictions mentioned. Later, however, some believers came from James with the result that many of the community stopped their table fellowship with Gentile believers. Peter and Barnabas, no lightweights in the church, were part of this withdrawal, which suggests that there may have been good arguments to act in this manner. At this point we have to remember Paul's penchant for strong language about those who disagreed with him. Tellingly, he has no victory to recount; Paul would have gladly related how he prevailed over his opponents, but here he does not because he cannot. In Paul's account, then, there are two stages to this debate over Gentile observance, the issue of circumcision and the issue of table fellowship.

The following chart will help clarify the differences between Paul's account in Galatians and Acts 15.

Galatians	Acts
Paul's initiative to go to Jerusalem —with Barnabas and Titus	Antioch appoints Barnabas and Paul
private meeting with "pillars" —Cephas, James, John	conference with apostles and elders —Peter, James —whole church
	Peter's speech reminds assembly of precedent of Cornelius (Acts 10–11)
Paul's mission to Gentiles recognized —Gentiles need not be circumcised —remember the poor	
	James's decision: Torah requirements for Gentiles (Lev 17–18)
	Barnabas and Paul sent back to Antioch with companions and letter
party from James (circumcision faction) —Cephas withdrew from eating with Gentiles —Barnabas and others with Cephas	
This version stresses Paul's independence, the validation of his Gentile mission; there are two events, the meeting in Jerusalem and the incident at Antioch.	This version stresses church unity and structure; Peter is initiator of Gentile mission; James expresses the community's decision—restrictions on Gentiles, especially regarding food. There is only one event, the meeting in Jerusalem; there is no tension between parties.

That there was in the early church a major dispute over circumcision and Gentile observance is not in question; nor is it in doubt that Paul was the initiator of a Gentile mission without circumcision. Either Luke did not know this or he made some changes. At any rate, he presented the resolution of these issues in the context of an assembly in Jerusalem, which seems to parallel a meeting recorded by Paul. For the sake of argument, if we take Paul's version at face value, we can make some suggestions as to why Luke might have had a different version. Let us review the differences.

Paul, in Acts 15, is a messenger and witness, not a major player (he has no "lines"),[1] while Peter and James are major characters. Paul has been brought into a church structure instead of being an independent apostle. Peter, as one of the original Twelve, is now credited with receiving Gentiles into the community, rather than Paul. Not simply a few leaders but the whole church is involved in the final decision, and that same decision is forwarded to the Gentile believers not only in Antioch, but also in Syria and Cilicia. There is no record of debate, of what kinds of opposition there might have been to any of the issues; there is no disagreement during and after the meeting. The decision is a harmonious one. The issue of observance of Torah restrictions for Gentiles is included in the final decision and letter, which is sent out by representatives of the Jerusalem church and not simply returned with Paul and Barnabas.

Why might Luke have written in this way? Throughout Acts, Luke is concerned about church unity and about authorization for decision making. Luke has a definite order in mind as he writes about the formation of the church, which is what he is doing. How did the community spread from Jerusalem? What happened when the Twelve were no longer available (by death or distance)? When and how were Gentiles allowed not to be circumcised? How did the church develop as it did? These are questions Luke is answering in his narrative. But is it history? This is the question modern readers

---

1. I often suggest to my students to pay attention to which characters have spoken lines and which ones remain silent in any given text. This technique can be revealing about the author's purposes.

have difficulty with: Either Luke wrote real history about what really happened or he was not writing history.

Acts 15 as History Writing

Some further clues can be found in the location of the episode of the Jerusalem meeting in the Book of Acts as a whole. It is never sufficient to try to understand a biblical text on its own; the context in which a passage occurs is also vital. That is certainly clear in the case of a single verse or a short passage, but here we are dealing with a longer passage, almost a chapter in Acts. Nonetheless, the context is revealing. If we think only in terms of numbers of chapters, it will not be immediately noticeable, but Acts 15 is the center of the whole book, both thematically and literally, and this is certainly not an accident. Consider the following: (a) in the first part of Acts, Peter has a major role, but after Chapter 15, Paul becomes the focal figure and Peter disappears from the scene; (b) the apostles (collectively) also disappear from the scene in the second part of Acts; (c) Jerusalem is the center and focus of the Christian movement before Chapter 15, whereas after that point, the focus has moved away from Jerusalem. As we read through Acts, a definite shift takes place after this incident. (There are further implications of this turning point that are not our concern at the moment, but are spelled out in the commentaries.) If Luke has set up his account in this way, what happened to history?

The Acts of the Apostles, as we are beginning to see, has its difficulties for the modern reader and for the modern historian. Some scholars are reluctant to call Acts a history in the first place; if it is a history, it is certainly not one according to modern ideas of history writing. Let us look at what Luke *did* write.

Acts is the second part of a two-volume work that was designed to be an organized narrative. The author of Luke and Acts sets this out at the beginning of the Gospel:

Since many have undertaken to set down an orderly
account of the events that have been fulfilled among us,
just as they were handed on to us by those who from the
beginning were eyewitnesses and servants of the word, I
too decided, after investigating everything carefully from
the very first, to write an orderly account for you, most
excellent Theophilus, so that you may know the truth
concerning the things about which you have been
instructed. (Luke 1:1–4)

The author of Acts is unknown, but is the same person who
wrote the third Gospel (names were not attached to the Gospels
until decades after their composition). According to tradition, the
author of both Gospel and Acts was Luke, mentioned by Paul as a
"fellow worker" in Phil 24. Luke is also mentioned in the letter to the
Colossians as "the beloved physician" (4:14) and in 2 Tim 4:11.
Aside from these references, nothing is known about him. Most
scholars doubt whether this Luke could be the author of Acts, partly
because the Gospel and Acts are anonymous, and partly because the
writer of Acts seems unaware of any of Paul's letters. These and
other problems call into question the traditional attribution of
authorship to Luke, the companion of Paul. It must be mentioned
that some scholars still accept the traditional identification of Luke
as the companion of Paul. And convention nevertheless continues to
use the name Luke for the author of the Gospel and Acts.

The author of Acts presumably had a variety of sources of information at his disposal, out of which he had to present his "orderly
account." Like any other historian or narrator, he also had an organizing principle. Luke's is revealed at the beginning of Acts, in the
words of Jesus to the disciples:

But you will receive power when the Holy Spirit has come
upon you; and you will be my witnesses *in Jerusalem, in
all Judea and Samaria, and to the ends of the earth.* (1:8)

Luke wants to show the spread of the gospel and the believing community outwards from Jerusalem and consequently works within a framework that is at one and the same time geographical, chronological, and theological.

Acts, accordingly, begins with the disciples still in Jerusalem with the risen Lord. Luke will continue to use his sacred geography as framework, showing the infant community spreading out from Jerusalem to the far reaches of the world. We can discern this plan at work: In the first few chapters, we see the believers in Jerusalem, coming into conflict with the authorities, gaining converts, and living as a community having but one heart and mind. Only after the death of Stephen do we learn of the disciples moving out from Jerusalem into Judea and Samaria (8:1, 4), followed by some anecdotes of their activities. Occasionally Luke reminds us of his geographical plan: "Meanwhile the church throughout Judea, Galilee, and Samaria had peace and was built up" (9:31).

After this, not surprisingly, comes the story of Peter's visit to Joppa, on the coast and so not part of Judea, Samaria, or Galilee. The church and the gospel are spreading outwards. With Chapter 13, the scene shifts farther afield to Antioch and Saul/Paul starts to enter the picture. Since it is from Antioch that Barnabas and Saul come with their question of circumcision, this brings us to the place where we started, the meeting at Jerusalem to decide whether and to what extent the Gentiles need follow Jewish observance. After this meeting, neither Peter nor any other apostle is mentioned again in Acts and instead the focus is on Paul, his teaching and his travels, which take him ultimately to Rome, the center of the first-century world.

Temporarily setting aside our modern discomfort at this kind of arrangement, we can see that Luke makes a logical case. Given Luke's conviction that God has worked in the world, *in history,* then it makes sense to use all the data he can gather, including religious belief. If God chose Jerusalem, as the scripture so often maintains, then there must be a historical as well as theological reason. The geography is sacred, not because Luke has an active imagination, but

29

because Luke's reading of scripture shows him the importance of the way the world is set out.

Jerusalem is the place from which God's revelation goes forth: In Luke's Gospel it is from Jerusalem that word of John's birth comes; it is in Jerusalem that both Anna and Simeon prophesy concerning Jesus; it is in Jerusalem that Jesus first appears learning from the teachers at the temple; it is in Jerusalem that Jesus dies, from Jerusalem that Jesus rises again; and when the risen Lord appears to the disciples in Jerusalem (but not in Galilee as in Matthew and John), he tells them to remain in the city (although in Mark and Matthew they are instructed to go to Galilee). In Acts, the Spirit comes upon the nascent believing community in Jerusalem, whither Jews from all over the world had gathered; it is from Jerusalem that the disciples go forth. Luke seems to follow the words of Isaiah: "For out of Zion shall go forth instruction, and the word of the LORD from Jerusalem" (Isa 2:3).

What about the Facts?

Let us suppose that by the 80s C.E., Luke has considerable information about the church. He does not have a scientifically accurate history of the Christian community to fall back on. He knows there are believers all over the Mediterranean (the Roman) world, in local communities. He knows that the disciples of Jesus were the source for the message about Jesus. He has names of leaders, stories about the various apostles. He knows how Roman governance works. He therefore needs to reconstruct from this uncoordinated information a logical sequence of events, an "orderly account." He chooses the material that will *also* speak theologically to his readers—fellow believers—about God's activity in the life of the church. He organizes the material in such a way that it emphasizes the centrality of Jerusalem, the authority of the apostles, and the unity of the church (Acts 2:42–47). He composes a history out of the material available to him.

It is important for Luke, therefore, that something as significant as release from Torah observance should have (must have) issued (a) from the mother church of Jerusalem, (b) from apostolic authority, and (c) as the decision of the whole community. Peter's role is essential. Whatever the factual situation—and it seems that Peter was in fact an ally of sorts of the "circumcision party"—it is necessary for Luke that Peter take the initiative in welcoming Gentiles into the community. Thus in Acts 9–10 Peter does just that. Paul's role is made subservient to the leadership of the Jerusalem community, so he does not just arrive at Jerusalem on his own initiative but is sent by the church of Antioch; he is chosen and appointed. Paul is also sent back, not even bearing the message himself, but accompanied by those appointed to bring the letter.

If, as is supposed, Luke did not have access to Paul's letters for consultation, nonetheless he does know of visits made to Jerusalem by Paul and that one visit included a debate over the issue of circumcision. He knows what a significant decision that was for the primitive church, as was the debate over table fellowship and the eating of "clean" and "unclean" foods. Luke has woven these data into a narrative that shows the unity of the church at large. Did such a public debate take place? Perhaps not, although there must at least have been debate throughout the Christian communities over the related issues of circumcision and table fellowship. This is clear from Paul's letters to Galatians and Corinthians (see 1 Cor 8 and 10). Luke has at least summarized the debate and the community consensus in this debate in Jerusalem.

The connection between circumcision and observance of other Jewish requirements is borne out by Paul's comments in Gal 2:11–14. Having just explained that his gospel without circumcision was deemed acceptable by the Jerusalem leadership, Paul then goes on to express his annoyance at Cephas (Peter) for not standing by his principles. When he came to Antioch, where Paul was working, Peter at first ate with Gentiles in accordance with the freedom allowed the Gentile converts, but quickly changed his ways when some of the "circumcision faction," as Paul calls them, arrived. Paul accused him of hypocrisy, of not acting consistently. Two connections may be noted in Paul's account. First, the believers who caused a disruption in the Antioch community are more conservative in their observance of Jewish requirements, apparently objecting to table fellowship with uncircumcised fellow believers. Second, they are associated with James (v. 12), a factor that perhaps gave them the weight to influence Peter and others to withdraw from table fellowship. Paul calls them "the circumcision faction," which reveals the connection between advocating circumcision for the Gentile believers and being conservative in ritual observance. Further, the association with James indicates that he was probably an observant member of the circumcision faction.

The decision that circumcision was not to be required of Gentiles is clear because that is the way Christianity developed, especially as it separated from Judaism. Luke, like Paul, represents the perspective that was finally adopted by the whole church. This viewpoint is also clear from Paul's letters, especially to the Galatians. The circumcision party was apparently still active, though, not only in the incident at Antioch but also among the Galatian churches. Whether or not dietary restrictions were placed on Gentiles is less clear, although there is some evidence to support this. The circumcision party represented closer continuity with the observant stream of Judaism, but the Christianity that became normative was associated with the non-observant stream.

Summary

What we find in Acts and Galatians are two different portraits of a major issue in the early years of Christianity. There is sometimes a tendency to forget that the first Christians were still Jews, who believed that they had met the Messiah (the Christ) in the person of Jesus of Nazareth. The first converts were simply other Jews who joined them in their conviction. Jews then, as Jews today, ranged from more conservative and observant of purity regulations to less traditional and observant. Some Jews were more urban and hellenized, more assimilated to the surrounding Greek culture of the eastern Mediterranean, while others remained more traditional or resistant to the Gentile world. There were also Gentile converts to Judaism and some men who had not undergone the final ritual of conversion, circumcision. Those who joined the Christian believers came from all sides of Judaism, so that they brought with them their traditional or non-traditional ways of life. Tensions between these interpretations of Judaism are reflected all through the New Testament (Acts 6, for example, deals with tension between "Hellenists" and "Hebrews"). It would be some decades before Christians would become separated from Judaism.

The issue of circumcision remained a thorny one for Gentile men wishing to convert. Some Christians simply assumed that a convert would become Jewish in order to accept Jesus as the Messiah, but others, like Paul, taught that Christ had broken through the old order to create a new creation, a new way of being in the Spirit. In this new creation, circumcision became irrelevant, if not actually obstructive. As we have already seen, circumcision brought with it other requirements; or, to put it differently, those who were adamant about the necessity of circumcision were also most insistent on complete observance. Both Acts and Paul's letter to the Galatians deal with this question.

We see in Acts not a simplistic record of the first Christians, but a complex narrative of tradition and ideology, which identifies the movements that composed the Christian community of Luke's day. Luke writes a history from the perspective of a non-observant Gentile reporting favorably on this development, and that of a believer in the unity of the church, such that all decisions have to be agreed by the whole. He is also a supporter of apostolic authority, both Peter's, as spokesman for the Twelve, and James's, as head of the Jerusalem church, which, because of its theological location in Luke's schema, is the source of revelation, through the working of the Spirit of Jesus in the community.

Luke has shaped his account of the Jerusalem meeting to include the most important decisions made by the infant church—

the decision not to require circumcision of Gentile believers and the decision to require a minimal observance of food regulations and marriage restrictions. Luke has placed this decision making in a conference of a full assembly to show the unity of Christians in Jerusalem as well as the agreement of Peter with James. Paul's presence at the meeting also implies his agreement. The meeting is set at a mid-point of Luke's account of the spread of Christian faith from Jerusalem to Rome (and by extension the Roman Empire). Thus, his point that the Christian community is united, centered in Jerusalem and harmoniously led by Peter, James of Jerusalem, and Paul, is well established. If we assume that Luke is the first one to pull together disparate bits of information about the early church (as opposed to the story of Jesus, whose framework he inherits from Mark), he needs to shape the material into a cohesive whole. The framework he uses is based on his (theological) premise of the fundamental unity of the early community, guided by the Holy Spirit. From this perspective, how else could such decisions have been made, if not with community consent and without friction? And since Jerusalem was the starting place of Christian faith, where else would such a decision have been made? His theological-geographical framework works well.

For Further Reading

Michael Cahill, "Bible Reading and Genre Recognition," *The Bible Today* (January 1999), 40–44.

Howard Clark Kee, *To Every Nation under Heaven: The Acts of the Apostles* (Harrisburg, PA: Trinity Press, 1997).

Mark Allan Powell, *What Are They Saying about Acts?* (Mahwah, NJ: Paulist Press, 1991), Chapter 5, "Reading Acts as History."

For Further Study

1. Find examples of different genres (types of writing) among the biblical books and discuss the importance of genre recognition.

2. Research and discuss the role of rhetoric in Paul's letters.

3. Explore the Jewish roots of the Christian church. What factors led to the separation of the Jesus movement from rabbinic Judaism?

4

WHAT HORSE?
PAUL'S CONVERSION IN ACTS

Most of us are familiar with the story of Paul's conversion on the road to Damascus, which is narrated in Chapter 9 of Acts. The story is told twice more in Acts, in speeches Paul makes after his arrest (22:3–21 and 26:1–23), indicating the significance that Luke assigned to this event. Yet Paul himself, in his own letters, says little about his conversion experience and nothing at all about the dramatic events on the Damascus road. Examining the way Luke presents Paul's conversion will reveal further aspects of biblical history writing. In this chapter we shall look at the first account in Acts 9, leaving the speeches for Chapter 5. As with the narrative of the church meeting in Jerusalem, it is to Paul's own words as the primary witness that we turn first.

Two Different Accounts

Gal 1:11–24

11. For I want you to know, brothers and sisters, that the gospel that was proclaimed by me is not of human origin; 12. for I did not receive it from a human source, nor was I taught it, but I received it through a revelation of Jesus Christ.

13. You have heard, no doubt, of my earlier life in Judaism. I was violently persecuting the church of God and was trying to destroy it. 14. I advanced in Judaism beyond many among my people of the same age, for I was

far more zealous for the traditions of my ancestors. 15. But when God, who had set me apart before I was born and called me through his grace, was pleased 16. to reveal his Son to me, so that I might proclaim him among the Gentiles, I did not confer with any human being, 17. nor did I go up to Jerusalem to those who were already apostles before me, but I went away at once into Arabia, and afterwards I returned to Damascus.

18. Then after three years I did go up to Jerusalem to visit Cephas and stayed with him fifteen days; 19. but I did not see any other apostle except James the Lord's brother. 20. In what I am writing to you, before God, I do not lie! 21. Then I went into the regions of Syria and Cilicia, 22. and I was still unknown by sight to the churches of Judea that are in Christ; 23. they only heard it said, "The one who formerly was persecuting us is now proclaiming the faith he once tried to destroy." 24. And they glorified God because of me.

As we examine Paul's own account of his conversion, we notice several interesting points. For one thing, Paul admits his earlier "persecution" of followers of Jesus, although he understandably does not go into detail. He also tells us of his zeal for Judaism,[1] a zeal that remains characteristic of Paul when he becomes a believer in Jesus as the Messiah. Further, Paul clearly understands the purpose of his experience to be his mission to the Gentiles. On the other hand, Paul unfortunately does not tell us what he means by "a revelation of Jesus Christ." Anyone who has read Acts assumes that Paul is referring to the Damascus road incident, but we do not know that for certain. And it is precisely that incident that we shall explore in this chapter.

As we saw in Chapter 2, Paul has a tendency to overstate his own position. Here we may have to modify his claim that he did not

---

1. Paul incidentally uses the term "Judaism," which was not yet common, found only here in the New Testament. Usually, the New Testament refers to the religion as "Israel."

receive his gospel from any "human source." At first glance, this might seem to mean that Paul learned the entire Christian message in his revelation, but in fact elsewhere he says that he is handing on certain traditions just as he received them (1 Cor 15:3–5, an early creedal formula), which points to his having had instruction in the gospel. The revelation that does not come from a human source probably refers to his mission to the Gentiles, rather than to his instruction into Christianity. For Paul, as for the other New Testament writers, the term *gospel* refers to the Christian message as it was preached and interpreted: There were as yet no writings known as gospels.

If we look more closely at what Paul has to say about visiting Jerusalem, we are struck by his statement that he did not go to Jerusalem immediately after his conversion experience (v. 17); in fact, he seems to emphasize his independence from the Jerusalem leadership. Why this was so is not clear, although Paul seems to suggest that his call took him, figuratively and literally, in another direction. After some time spent in "Arabia,"[2] Paul returned to Damascus. Paul does not mention any other home base, and his simple comment about his return suggests this was where he normally lived. By the time Galatians was written, however, Paul had made two trips to Jerusalem and was then living in Antioch (2:11). The second trip to Jerusalem (48 or 49 C.E.) is the one we have explored in the previous chapter, and the first one probably occurred about ten to twelve years earlier (37–39 C.E.). Paul's conversion seems to have taken place very early in the history of the Christian community, perhaps 32 or 33 C.E.

To summarize, Paul lets us know that, after "violently persecuting the church of God," he had some kind of experience in which "God revealed his Son" to him, and through which he understood that he was to bring the Christian message to the Gentiles. He gives us no details and makes no reference to the Damascus road event. Let us turn, then, to the description that Luke gives us in Acts.

---

2. "Arabia," mentioned only in Gal 1:17 and 4:25 in the New Testament, is a general term for the lands south of modern Amman (Jordan) and southern Negev (Israel), and is not to be identified with modern Saudi Arabia.

Acts 9:1–30

Meanwhile Saul, still breathing threats and murder against the disciples of the Lord, went to the high priest 2. and asked him for letters to the synagogues at Damascus, so that if he found any who belonged to the Way, men or women, he might bring them bound to Jerusalem. 3. Now as he was going along and approaching Damascus, suddenly a light from heaven flashed around him. 4. He fell to the ground and heard a voice saying to him, "Saul, Saul, why do you persecute me?" 5. He asked, "Who are you, Lord?" The reply came, "I am Jesus, whom you are persecuting. 6. But get up and enter the city, and you will be told what you are to do." 7. The men who were traveling with him stood speechless because they heard the voice but saw no one. 8. Saul got up from the ground, and though his eyes were open, he could see nothing; so they led him by the hand and brought him into Damascus. 9. For three days he was without sight, and neither ate nor drank.

10. Now there was a disciple in Damascus named Ananias. The Lord said to him in a vision, "Ananias." He answered, "Here I am, Lord." 11. The Lord said to him, "Get up and go to the street called Straight, and at the house of Judas look for a man of Tarsus named Saul. At this moment he is praying, 12. and he has seen in a vision a man named Ananias come in and lay his hands on him so that he might regain his sight." 13. But Ananias answered, "Lord, I have heard from many about this man, how much evil he has done to your saints in Jerusalem; 14. and here he has authority from the chief priests to bind all who invoke your name." 15. But the Lord said to him, "Go, for he is an instrument whom I have chosen to bring my name before Gentiles and kings and before the people of Israel; 16. I myself will show him how much he must suffer for

the sake of my name." 17. So Ananias went and entered the house. He laid his hands on Saul and said, "Brother Saul, the Lord Jesus, who appeared to you on your way here, has sent me so that you may regain your sight and be filled with the Holy Spirit." 18. And immediately something like scales fell from his eyes, and his sight was restored. Then he got up and was baptized, 19. and after taking some food, he regained his strength.

For several days he was with the disciples in Damascus, 20. and immediately he began to proclaim Jesus in the synagogues, saying, "He is the Son of God." 21. All who heard him were amazed and said, "Is not this the man who made havoc in Jerusalem among those who invoked this name? And has he not come here for the purpose of bringing them bound before the chief priests?" 22. Saul became increasingly more powerful and confounded the Jews who lived in Damascus by proving that Jesus was the Messiah. 23. After some time had passed, the Jews plotted to kill him, 24. but their plot became known to Saul. They were watching the gates day and night so that they might kill him; 25. but his disciples took him by night and let him down through an opening in the wall, lowering him in a basket.

26. When he had come to Jerusalem, he attempted to join the disciples; and they were all afraid of him, for they did not believe that he was a disciple. 27. But Barnabas took him, brought him to the apostles, and described for them how on the road he had seen the Lord, who had spoken to him, and how in Damascus he had spoken boldly in the name of Jesus. 28. So he went in and out among them in Jerusalem, speaking boldly in the name of the Lord. 29. He spoke and argued with the Hellenists; but they were attempting to kill him. 30. When the believers learned of it, they brought him down to Caesarea and sent him off to Tarsus.

So many artistic representations of Paul's conversion on the road to Damascus show Paul on (or falling off!) a horse that it has become a "fact" and a byword. You will have noticed, however, that there is no horse in this account. (Nor for that matter are there any soldiers, who also turn up in depictions of this incident.) This sums up the way we remember dramatic narratives—not by literal adherence to the text but by an amalgam of memory and imagination. We picture in our minds what might have happened, or draw on the art we have seen, so that very quickly the image becomes entwined with the text and is itself a commentary on, or an interpretation of, the text. Even without the horse, however, the text tells a dramatic story.

To summarize the events in Acts 9, we notice that as Paul approaches the city he is surprised by a light from heaven, at which he falls to the ground. Paul then hears a voice, which is also heard by his companions (v. 7). As Paul rises from the ground, he finds that he is blind and has to be led into the city, where Ananias heals him. Paul is baptized and immediately begins preaching that Jesus is Son of God. After some time (v. 23) Paul has to make his escape from the city and goes to Jerusalem, where, after some initial misgivings on the part of the community, he begins preaching there too, not without opposition. Later, for his own security, Paul is sent away from Jerusalem to Caesarea.

Having just read Paul's brief version of events in Galatians, however, you will also have noticed some differences from one account to the other. The most obvious difference is that Paul is named Saul in Acts until 13:9, where the name change takes place. (For the sake of convenience we shall continue to call him Paul.) Next, whereas Paul makes it very clear that he spent some time in Arabia before returning to Damascus (Gal 1:18), Acts lacks this information and gives the impression that Paul went to Jerusalem fairly soon after his conversion and spent some time there. Another discrepancy occurs in the reference to Paul's escape from Damascus, lowered down the city wall in a basket, related in Acts 9 but not in Galatians. Paul does speak of this escape elsewhere (2 Cor 11:32–33), but at that point does not specify when it happened, although Luke's version presents the most likely occasion. More significantly, Paul says that he was about to be arrested by the king, Aretas, who had a watch put on the city. In Acts, Paul's need to escape is attributed to the hostility of the Jews, who were watching the gates.

Still, Acts and Paul are largely in accord. Paul says of himself that he was well educated and observant in the Jewish tradition; that he attacked the new movement violently; and that by a "revelation" God called him to proclaim the good news among the Gentiles. What is lacking in Luke's version is Paul's sojourn in Arabia before returning to Damascus. Both Acts and Paul refer to his departure from that city and subsequent visit to Jerusalem, although with different details. Luke in Acts presents a dramatized reconstruction of events.

Luke's Reconstruction

Whatever information Luke had about Paul has certainly been reworked and woven into the overall portrait of the church's early years. Luke was not writing a biography of Paul; Paul is one (albeit major) personage in the history, whose story is only part of the whole. Luke is the one who creates this history for succeeding generations, the one who gave it its first shape. We can suggest what his raw material was. At the very least, Luke knew of Paul's conversion after severely persecuting members of the church. It must have been common knowledge that Paul had been educated as an observant Jew (as Paul himself writes in Gal 1:14) and that he had at first been regarded with suspicion; other Christians must have taken some persuading that he had reversed his position and was now a committed follower. (Paul hints at this in Gal 1:22–23, but presents it in more positive terms.) Ananias was probably a well-known figure in the Damascus church and may indeed have been the one to baptize Paul and introduce him to the rest of the community. Luke knew of Paul's escape from Damascus at some point and of Paul's subsequent visit to Jerusalem. He probably knew that Paul had visions, but not their content or occasion, except perhaps that they had something to do with Paul's mission to the Gentiles.

It was Luke's task to incorporate what he knew of Paul into his history. This would include filling in the blanks with logical assumptions and dramatizing the bare facts both for effect and to make a (theological) point. This method was typical of ancient history writing. There are several features that reveal Luke's reworking of the account of Paul's call experience.[3] First, the event takes place on the road, on a journey, a motif that Luke uses well. Much of the Gospel of Luke presents Jesus on the road from Galilee to Jerusalem; starting at 9:51 and apparent frequently thereafter (9:57; 10:1, 38; 13:22; 17:11, etc.), this motif becomes even more noticeable as Jesus gets closer to Jerusalem. Traveling occurs in several of Luke's narratives, from the birth and childhood of Jesus (Luke 1–2) to the parable of the Good Samaritan (Luke 10:30–36). Significantly, one of the post-resurrection appearances takes place on the road out of Jerusalem, when the risen Jesus walks with two disciples and then makes himself known to them in the breaking of the bread (Luke 24:13–32). Notice in this connection the statement of Barnabas in Acts 9:27, which echoes the report of the disciples who returned to Jerusalem to tell the others what had happened to them on the road (Luke 24:35). In Acts, Paul's missionary travels fit well with Luke's liking for the journey motif. In this context it is not surprising that Luke would have set this experience on the road.

A second interesting feature of this account is the two-fold vision. Paul and Ananias each have a revelatory experience that correlates with the other; Paul is told to go into the city, where in the meantime Ananias through a vision is being prepared to heal and baptize Paul. Ananias is actually having a vision of a vision, a technique that appears in the classical, but not Jewish, literature of the time; its purpose is to show divine intervention in events. Although Paul's call experience is apparently a voice only, Ananias is told that Paul is having a vision of him, Ananias, coming to heal him. In the next narrative in Acts, Cornelius the centurion and Peter also have matching visions. Cornelius is told in his vision to send for Simon

---

3. Most commentators think that Luke had a traditional account of Paul's conversion to work with.

Peter, who was staying in Joppa (10:3–6).[4] While the messengers "were on their journey and approaching the city" (10:9), Peter in his turn has a vision of clean and unclean foods (10:10–16). Between them, the visions prepare for the acceptance of Gentiles, and the repetition of them in speeches by Cornelius and Peter emphasizes the importance of this step in the church's development. Ananias's vision prepares for the mistrust Paul will encounter but also announces Paul's role in the mission to the Gentiles. In both cases the visions interact with each other to give a full presentation of the message. In fact, it is the vision of Ananias that tells us of Paul's mission; in the narrative to that point, Paul himself does not yet know. Patterning of this sort reveals the author's hand at work, whether reworking a received tradition or creating a dramatic episode.

Are the visions historical? Paul's initial experience is not strictly a vision, although that is how it is often interpreted and described. A bright light transfixes him and he hears a voice; nowhere does Luke or Paul say that he actually saw Jesus at this point. Further, the details are typical of such visions: There is a light, the recipient falls down and is the only one to experience the revelation. Although Paul does not refer to this particular incident in any of his letters, he does speak of having had visions (1 Cor 15:8; 2 Cor 12:1–7). A later writer, such as Luke, might well have logically surmised that such a vision occurred at the key moments of Paul's life, beginning with his call. On the other hand, here we have echoes of other prophetic visions narrated in the Old Testament. Saul/Paul and Ananias are addressed by name, just as were Moses at the theophany of the burning bush (Exod 3:4) and Samuel in the sanctuary at Shiloh (1 Sam 3:4, 6, 10). Ananias responds as Samuel did, "Here I am, Lord." These visions express the prophet's call to serve Yahweh. Similarly Paul's experience also has elements of a prophetic call, as well as a life-transforming conversion.

In both the Gospel and Acts, Luke emphasizes the role of the prophet. Jesus himself is presented as prophet in his life and words in the Gospel, while in Acts the activity of the believers frequently

---

4. Cf. also the two-fold angelic visitation to Zachary and Mary in Luke 1:8–20, 26–38.

echoes that of the great prophets of Israel. Paul's conversion and the later account of his temple vision (Acts 22:17–21) reflect the Old Testament's prophets' call to vocation. Luke presents Paul like a prophet who has had a revelatory vision directing him to his mission—like Moses, Amos, or Isaiah. At the same time, Luke models Paul on Jesus, especially in his arrest and trial. Like Jesus, Paul is in darkness for three days before being restored to light; like Jesus, Paul has to suffer (9:16), experience hostility from his own people who seek to kill him (9:23), is arrested (21:31–35) and brought to trial before the Jewish (23:1–5) and Roman authorities (24:1–23; 25:6–12). As the patterns emerge, Luke's hand in shaping the narrative is more clearly seen.

The hand of Luke may also be seen in the parallel structure of the period in Damascus and the period in Jerusalem. In each case there is reluctance to accept Paul (Ananias in Damascus, the disciples in Jerusalem), reassurance from the Lord in one situation and Barnabas in the other, and a plot against Paul followed by an escape. In both cases, Paul is subordinated to the church, baptized (and by implication instructed) by Ananias, under the aegis of Barnabas and the apostles in Jerusalem. Parallel narratives, like parallel visions, are characteristic of Luke, the most familiar probably being the dual birth narratives of John the Baptist and Jesus in Luke 1–2, and less familiar the twin parables of lost sheep and lost coin (Luke 15:3–10), the latter found only in Luke. On a larger scale, in Acts the mission of Paul is paralleled to that of Peter, and his life to that of Jesus, especially in his arrest and trials.

The omission of Arabia may simply have been the result of lack of information on Luke's part, or it may have been deemed irrelevant to Luke's history. Although Paul himself does not tell us precisely when he had to escape from Damascus, saying only that he went to Jerusalem and then into Syria and Cilicia (Gal 1:18–21), this would be the logical moment for it. It is not surprising, however, that Luke develops the time spent in Jerusalem. Although Paul says that he stayed only fourteen days and apparently avoided the community as a whole, Luke has assumed that Paul was being introduced to the believers, especially the apostles, and engaged in preaching. This accords well with Luke's insistence on the centrality of the Jerusalem church and the authority of the apostles. Without access to the letter to the Galatians, it must have seemed logical to Luke that Paul could not have proceeded without the knowledge of the apostles, and he has interpreted Paul's visit as a moment of validation. Notice how Acts describes it: Barnabas introduces Paul *to the apostles,* and vouches for this newcomer who has a frightening reputation (Acts 9:26–27). Thus Paul is able to move freely in the community in Jerusalem, having the approbation of the apostolic leadership.

Acts 9 in Context

The narratives about Paul, although of major importance, are only part of the larger history. As we saw in the previous chapter, Luke arranged his material in Acts to show how the Christian community spread outwards from Jerusalem "to the ends of the earth" (1:8). A quick survey of the first few chapters reveals the primitive church in Jerusalem, drawing believers from the Jewish community (2:5,41, 6:7; etc.), in increasing numbers (2:41, 47; 3:4; 6:7; etc.), attending the temple (for example, 3:1; 5:42), and living as a community (see 2:42–47 and 4:32–35 for summaries of church life).

A shift takes place after the martyrdom of Stephen at the end of Chapter 7, when the community is forced to flee the city for outlying areas. This is expressed in terms of Luke's geographical framework, established in 1:8: "You will be my witnesses in Jerusalem, in all Judea and Samaria, and to the ends of the earth." The action moves away from Jerusalem with the disciples: "all except the apostles were scattered throughout the countryside of Judea and Samaria," proclaiming the good news as they went (8:1, 4; cf. 1:8). Philip is one who brings the gospel into Samaria before being sent to the Gaza road, then going to Azotus and finally Caesarea (on the Mediterranean coast). Jerusalem, however, remains the center for the apostles (8:1, 25).

At the end of Paul's conversion episode, Luke summarizes the spread of the church so far:

> Meanwhile the church throughout Judea, Galilee, and Samaria had peace and was built up. Living in the fear of the Lord and in the comfort of the Holy Spirit, it increased in numbers. (9:31)

The first part of the community's expansion has been completed. After this, Luke will narrate episodes that involve Peter, who also travels around (9:32), away from Judea towards the coast, finally staying in Joppa. From Joppa, Peter will go to the Roman centurion Cornelius in Caesarea (Acts 10). Luke will again refer to his framework in 11:1, stating that the disciples back in Judea learned of the Gentiles' acceptance, and in 11:19, where he will then reveal that the disciples have also been traveling into Phoenicia (along the coast but further north than Caesarea); Cyprus, a nearby island; and Antioch, inland in Syria.

Into this context of geographical expansion Luke sets a series of conversions of unlikely candidates: Simon the magician (8:9–24), the Ethiopian eunuch (8:26–38), Saul the murderous persecutor of the disciples, and Cornelius the Gentile. The purpose of these conversions is to show how God takes the initiative in opening up the church beyond the immediate circle of Jerusalem and Jews. Simon and the Ethiopian are both baptized by Philip as he makes his way through Samaria to Caesarea (8:5, 40). Simon is an example of how well the good news is received in Samaria, traditionally hostile to Jews, while the Ethiopian, returning home from Jerusalem, suggests the spread of the gospel far to the south. The hostile Saul "breathing threats and murder" is converted to Saul (later Paul) the preacher, showing how the power of the gospel can transform an enemy into a believer. Finally, the conversion of Cornelius opens the community to the Gentiles. The church spreads not only geographically but also inclusively: Jews, Samaritans, Gentiles, foes—all are accepted into the believing community.

Moreover, Luke makes it clear throughout that this is entirely God's initiative: An angel directs Philip to meet the Ethiopian (8:26); Saul has his visionary experience while he is in the midst of seeking out believers for punishment; and Cornelius, a God-fearer, is directed to send for Peter in a vision of an angel, while Peter has his own vision directing him to accept Gentiles (10:3–6, 9–16, 34–35). Each of these actors is instrumental at key junctures in the spread of the church: Philip is responsible for the gospel's acceptance in Samaria and beyond, Saul will become Paul, Cornelius and Peter together reveal that the Spirit of God is extended to Gentiles without reservation. Just as the prophets of old were called and directed by God, so too are the members of the new community.

Acts 9, then, has been set into this context not only to narrate the fact of Paul's conversion but also to show how it relates to the bigger picture. From Chapter 8, when the disciples are forced to leave Jerusalem—providentially it would seem, since that is the impetus for the spread of the gospel—to the end of Chapter 9, the church spreads through Judea, Galilee, and Samaria, as Jesus told the apostles in 1:8. After that, the church spreads further and further into Gentile territory. Paul's conversion is set just before the point where the Gentiles are first received into the community. Although Paul is known as the apostle to the Gentiles, in Acts priority is given to Peter as the first to accept non-Jews (10:28, 34–35).

Summary

Earlier, we saw how Luke dealt with major questions in the early church—circumcision and table fellowship for Gentiles—correlating diverse items of information into a coherent narrative by applying his assumption of the centrality of the Jerusalem leadership. In this chapter, we have seen Luke using his geographical framework to show the spread of the Christian message and community from its original center of Jerusalem. Not only is the movement of Christianity away from Jerusalem; it is also an increasingly inclusive movement, evidence that God's salvation is universal. This, too, is a character of Luke's Gospel, beginning with the angelic proclamation at the birth of Jesus ("I am bringing you good news of great joy for all the people"; Luke 2:10). Throughout the Gospel, Luke reveals that the good news of forgiveness and salvation is available for poor and rich, devout and sinner, women and men.

Bare facts are not history. Any historian sets the data into a context that interprets the events, proposes relationships, and provides explanations. Luke has done just that: He has composed a flowing narrative in which information has been arranged into a logical sequence, informed by a theological perspective. Again, we must remember that Luke was, as far as we know, the first to compose a comprehensive story of what happened, which he had to reconstruct out of a collection of disparate information, such as anecdotes, names of individuals and places, and other data. There was already an account of the life of Jesus, namely the Gospel of Mark (even if Matthew's Gospel had been already written, it seems that Luke did not know it), and a collection of sayings of Jesus,[5] both of which Luke was able to use in his own Gospel. For the story of the church, however, Luke would have had to start from scratch. Some of his material, if not much of it, must have been oral tradition rather than written reports. Where he had little or no information, he had to construct what seemed logical, what he knew and what he believed must have happened. He knew that Jerusalem was the starting place, and it was clear to Luke fifty years later that the church was now established all over the Roman Empire. He certainly had some information about well-known or significant individuals such as Peter, James the brother of the Lord, and Saul/Paul. If indeed Luke did not have access to any of Paul's letters, he certainly knew much about the man and his life. Finally, Luke used theological assumptions—his beliefs about the Risen One, the power of the Spirit, and the universality of salvation—to guide the ordering of his material.

---

5. A sayings collection, known as "Q," is generally supposed by scholars to have been in existence at the time of Luke's writing. Both Matthew and Luke availed themselves of this material, incorporating it into their respective Gospels.

Out of this, Luke fashioned a narrative that speaks as much to faith as to historical interests.

Just as a painting of Paul falling off his horse is a visual interpretation of what happened on the road to Damascus, so too is Luke's dramatic account an interpretation of Paul's conversion from being a violent opponent of the new Christian movement to being one of its most fearless witnesses. This was a remarkable moment in the history of the fledgling church, that an enemy could be transformed so completely into an apostle whose work took the gospel ever farther afield. For Luke, this was none other than the work of God, the ultimate author of history. The narrative of Acts 9 is spun through with the threads of Luke's language of journey, prophetic call, sight and blindness, and bold witness. Nor is Luke done with Paul's witness of conversion. In the words of the Lord to Ananias, Paul is a chosen instrument who will bring the name of Jesus "before Gentiles and kings and before the people of Israel." This Paul does not only in his missionary travels but also in his defense speeches before the people of Jerusalem in Acts 22 and before the Roman governor and King Agrippa in Acts 26, to which we now turn.

For Further Reading

Charles T. Dougherty, "Did Paul Fall off a Horse?" *Bible Review* XIII (August 1997), 42–44.

Daniel Marguerat, "Saul's Conversion (Acts 9, 22, 26) and the Multiplication of Narrative in Acts" in C.M. Tuckett, ed., *Luke's Literary Achievement* (Sheffield, England: Sheffield Academic Press, 1995), pp. 127–155.

Mark Allan Powell, *What Are They Saying About Acts?* (Mahwah, NJ: Paulist Press, 1991), Chapter 6, "Reading Acts as Literature."

For Further Study

1. Read Luke 24:44–52 and Acts 1:1–11 and compare the two passages. What is the purpose of the author's repetition of the same event?

2. Read Acts 2:1–13. What difference does it make to think of this description as a dramatization of a theological statement rather than a factual report?

5

Light and Blindness:
Paul's Conversion in His Speeches

Luke's threefold inclusion of Paul's conversion scene has been explained in a variety of ways. The versions have been seen as the result of different sources used by Luke, as superficial variations, and even as carelessness in Luke's writing style. But the relationship of the narrative of Acts 9 to the speeches of Acts 22 and 26 is more complex and deliberate, part of Luke's narrative art. The repetition of this scene indicates that Luke considered the event to be exceptionally significant. Paul's role in Luke's history is clearly of major import since he is the focus of the second part of the book, so it is no surprise that his conversion should be a focal point for the historian, worthy of retelling.

Paul's First Speech:
His Defense before the Jews of Jerusalem

The immediate context for the first speech is Paul's return to Jerusalem after extensive traveling. This time, Paul is warmly received by the community, but the shadow of the circumcision issue still looms over him (21:17–31). To complete observance of a vow, Paul goes to the temple (v. 26), where the crowd is roused to seize Paul, on the grounds that he taught against the traditions of Judaism (vv. 27–28). Paul is rescued from the mob, now ready to kill him, but is arrested by the Roman tribune (v. 33) and then allowed to address the crowd (v. 40).

Acts 22:1–22

1. "Brothers and fathers, listen to the defense that I now make before you." 2. When they heard him addressing them in Hebrew, they became even more quiet.

Then he said: 3. "I am a Jew, born in Tarsus in Cilicia, but brought up in this city at the feet of Gamaliel, educated strictly according to our ancestral law, being zealous for God, just as all of you are today. 4. I persecuted this Way up to the point of death by binding both men and women and putting them in prison, 5. as the high priest and the whole council of elders can testify about me. From them I also received letters to the brothers in Damascus, and I went there in order to bind those who were there and to bring them back to Jerusalem for punishment.

6. "While I was on my way and approaching Damascus, about noon a great light from heaven suddenly shone about me. 7. I fell to the ground and heard a voice saying to me, 'Saul, Saul, why are you persecuting me?' 8. I answered, 'Who are you, Lord?' Then he said to me, 'I am Jesus of Nazareth whom you are persecuting.' 9. Now those who were with me saw the light but did not hear the voice of the one who was speaking to me. 10. I asked, 'What am I to do, Lord?' The Lord said to me, 'Get up and go to Damascus; there you will be told everything that has been assigned to you to do.' 11. Since I could not see because of the brightness of that light, those who were with me took my hand and led me to Damascus.

12. "A certain Ananias, who was a devout man according to the law and well spoken of by all the Jews living there, 13. came to me; and standing beside me, he said, 'Brother Saul, regain your sight!' In that very hour I regained my sight and saw him. 14. Then he said, 'The God of our ancestors has chosen you to know his will, to see the Righteous One and to hear his own voice; 15. for

you will be his witness to all the world of what you have seen and heard. 16. And now why do you delay? Get up, be baptized, and have your sins washed away, calling on his name.'

17. "After I had returned to Jerusalem and while I was praying in the temple, I fell into a trance 18. and saw Jesus saying to me, 'Hurry and get out of Jerusalem quickly, because they will not accept your testimony about me.' 19. And I said, 'Lord, they themselves know that in every synagogue I imprisoned and beat those who believed in you. 20. And while the blood of your witness Stephen was shed, I myself was standing by, approving and keeping the coats of those who killed him.' 21. Then he said to me, 'Go, for I will send you far away to the Gentiles.'" 22. Up to this point they listened to him, but then they shouted, "Away with such a fellow from the earth! For he should not be allowed to live."

The story is probably familiar, but there are (by now anticipated) discrepancies. Having introduced himself to his audience, Paul proceeds to relate what happened on the road to Damascus. The essential points are repeated exactly: the appearance of the light, the voice asking, "Saul, Saul, why are you persecuting me?" and the identification of Jesus "whom you are persecuting." In this version, however, Paul says that his companions saw the light but did not hear the voice, in contrast to Acts 9, which says they heard the voice but saw nothing. Furthermore, after he relates his baptism, Paul jumps immediately to his return to Jerusalem, omitting any reference to his escape from Damascus. Moreover, he expands on his time in Jerusalem by relating that while praying in the temple he had a vision of Jesus, who told him to leave the city. At this point in the speech, the crowd interrupts with shouts of hostility.

It is immediately clear that Paul is speaking to fellow Jews and his speech is directed accordingly, addressing his listeners as "fathers and brothers." He speaks in "Hebrew" (that is, Aramaic, the language in use among the people), introducing himself as a Jew who has been educated "strictly according to our ancestral law," that is, as one trained in exact observance of Jewish traditions, and he emphasizes his previous enmity towards the new Christians. Ananias is now described as "a devout man *according to the law*," again a reference to traditional observance, and someone who is moreover "well spoken of by all the Jews" in Damascus. He is also now described as saying, "the God of our ancestors has chosen you" instead of "the Lord Jesus...has sent me," which would be more readily understood by the Jews to whom Paul speaks. More precisely, the reported version of Ananias's speech is much more specific than in Acts 9: Compare

> "Brother Saul, the Lord Jesus who has appeared to you on your way here, has sent me so that you may regain your sight and be filled with the Holy Spirit." (9:17)

with

> "The God of our ancestors has chosen you to know his will, to see the Righteous One and to hear his own voice; for you will be his witness to all the world of what you have seen and heard. And now why do you delay? Get up, be baptized, and have your sins washed away, calling on his name." (22:14–16)

There is no suggestion of any hesitation on Paul's part in Acts 9; this exhortation is added as a model for the Jews who are listening to Paul—*they* are the ones who should be baptized without delay. Paul thus retells his story in a way that will witness to his message as well as relate what happened to him.

In this context, Paul adds a report about a vision in the temple. In this way, Paul demonstrates his Jewish piety, by his prayer and by his attendance in the temple. The resemblance to the prophetic vision of Isaiah (Isa 6) is stronger: Paul reminds Jesus of his former attacks on the believers, Isaiah had protested his unworthiness (Isa 6:5); Isaiah was sent to the people Israel, Paul is sent to the

Gentiles. The commission comes directly from Jesus (v. 21), whereas in the first account only Ananias had been informed of Paul's mission (9:15). Finally, as Paul is relating how the vision told him he would be sent "far away" from Jerusalem to the Gentiles, the context of Chapter 22 is precisely that: He is at the beginning of events that will end in his removal from Jerusalem for Rome.

The speech as a whole emphasizes Paul's Jewishness and fidelity to the temple. The effect is to demonstrate that belief in Jesus is in continuity with Judaism, not in opposition to it. He is defending himself against the accusation that he "is teaching everyone everywhere against our people, our law, and this place [the temple]" (21:28); his speech is exactly that, a defense—apologia (22:1). The speech identifies both Paul and Ananias as devout Jews, and Paul's experience in the temple—the most sacred place—validates his claims.

Paul's Second Speech: His Defense before Agrippa

Paul's second speech occurs in Caesarea before the Roman governor Festus and king Agrippa (Herod Agrippa II). Festus had inherited Paul from the previous governor, Felix, who had simply left him in prison (24:27). All this followed from his arrest at the temple, the occasion for the previous speech. Since then, Paul had claimed Roman citizenship (22:25–29), had been brought before the council (22:30–23:10), and had been taken from Jerusalem to Caesarea to avoid an ambush (23:12–35). In Chapter 24, Paul was charged as an agitator before Felix, then governor, who finally did nothing. At this point, Paul had already appeared once before Festus and had claimed his right to be tried in Rome (25:9–12). Agrippa and his sister Berenice were in town to give Festus an official welcome to the province, when Festus decided that Paul would be of interest to the king. This second speech is addressed primarily to Agrippa.

Acts 26:1–24

1. Agrippa said to Paul, "You have permission to speak for yourself." Then Paul stretched out his hand and began to defend himself:

2. "I consider myself fortunate that it is before you, King Agrippa, I am to make my defense today against all the accusations of the Jews, 3. because you are especially familiar with all the customs and controversies of the Jews; therefore I beg of you to listen to me patiently. 4. All the Jews know my way of life from my youth, a life spent from the beginning among my own people and in Jerusalem. 5. They have known for a long time, if they are willing to testify, that I have belonged to the strictest sect of our religion and lived as a Pharisee. 6. And now I stand here on trial on account of my hope in the promise made by God to our ancestors, 7. a promise that our twelve tribes hope to attain, as they earnestly worship day and night. It is for this hope, your Excellency, that I am accused by Jews! 8. Why is it thought incredible by any of you that God raises the dead?

9. "Indeed, I myself was convinced that I ought to do many things against the name of Jesus of Nazareth. 10. And that is what I did in Jerusalem; with authority received from the chief priests, I not only locked up many of the saints in prison, but I also cast my vote against them when they were being condemned to death. 11. By punishing them often in all the synagogues I tried to force them to blaspheme; and since I was so furiously enraged at them, I pursued them even to foreign cities.

12. "With this in mind, I was traveling to Damascus with the authority and commission of the chief priests, 13. when at midday along the road, your Excellency, I saw a light from heaven, brighter than the sun, shining around me and my companions. 14. When we had all fallen to the

ground, I heard a voice saying to me in the Hebrew language, 'Saul, Saul, why are you persecuting me? It hurts you to kick against the goads.' 15. I asked, 'Who are you, Lord?' The Lord answered, 'I am Jesus whom you are persecuting. 16. But get up and stand on your feet; for I have appeared to you for this purpose, to appoint you to serve and testify to the things in which you have seen me and to those in which I will appear to you. 17. I will rescue you from your people and from the Gentiles—to whom I am sending you 18. to open their eyes so that they may turn from darkness to light and from the power of Satan to God, so that they may receive forgiveness of sins and a place among those who are sanctified by faith in me.'

19. "After that, King Agrippa, I was not disobedient to the heavenly vision, 20. but declared first to those in Damascus, then in Jerusalem and throughout the countryside of Judea, and also to the Gentiles, that they should repent and turn to God and do deeds consistent with repentance. 21. For this reason the Jews seized me in the temple and tried to kill me. 22. To this day I have had help from God, and so I stand here, testifying to both small and great, saying nothing but what the prophets and Moses said would take place: 23. that the Messiah must suffer, and that, by being the first to rise from the dead, he would proclaim light both to our people and to the Gentiles." 24. While he was making this defense, Festus exclaimed, "You are out of your mind, Paul! Too much learning is driving you insane!"

This is another defense speech (*apologia*, v. 2), undertaken by Paul technically before the Roman governor Festus, but addressed to Agrippa, a local king (Herod Agrippa II, descended from Herod the Great). In this speech, Paul remarks that since Agrippa is acquainted with Jewish matters, he can be expected to understand Paul's arguments. Having given a fuller explanation of why he was traveling to Damascus, Paul relates his experience in terms very similar to the first account. The essential elements are exactly the same: the light, the voice from heaven saying, "Saul, Saul, why are you persecuting me?" and the identification, "I am Jesus whom you are persecuting."

Once again, however, we see some odd divergences from previous accounts. Whereas, in the previous speech to the Jews in Jerusalem, Paul felt it necessary to introduce himself as a Jew from Tarsus, now he claims that all the Jews know that he had been brought up in Jerusalem as a strict Pharisee—and that they have known this for a long time (v. 5). The claim is that Paul was well known as a Jew in Jerusalem, something that does not come through in Acts 22. On the other hand, Paul would have had to be in high esteem to acquire authority from the chief priests to pursue followers of Jesus beyond Judea into "foreign cities." In this, the speech is internally consistent. Paul's previous hostility to the believers is more detailed than before and serves to underline the amazing nature of his call and mission by the same Jesus he was persecuting.

A new element is the addition of a summary of Paul's missionary preaching, from Damascus to Jerusalem, and then through Judea and beyond to the Gentiles. This follows Paul's activity as Luke has described it in Acts, but does not easily fit with Paul's own comments in his letters. It also conforms to Luke's understanding of how the gospel has spread. Paul now claims that the reason for his arrest is his preaching of repentance and resurrection, and he appeals to the scriptures ("the prophets and Moses") to support his teaching. His final point is that the Messiah "would proclaim light to our people and to the Gentiles" (v. 23).

In the previous speech, there was considerable emphasis on Paul's Jewishness. Here, there are comments that show Paul relating to his Greek-speaking audience. In his description of what happened on the road, he explains that the voice addressed him in Hebrew (Aramaic), but then he adds a proverb to what the Lord has said, "It hurts you to kick against the goads" (v. 14). The proverb, however, is a Greek saying, well known in the classical world and therefore familiar to Paul's listeners, but certainly not Jewish! The adaptation of a speech to its audience is a technique typical of ancient history writing.

But more importantly, Paul's speech emphasizes the power of God. His very conversion from violent persecutor to zealous preacher is witness to God's power at work. The light Paul describes is brighter than the sun (v. 13), evidence of its heavenly origin. Paul says he could not disobey a divine vision (v. 19), itself a sign of God's intervention, and he speaks of resurrection (vv. 8, 23), the ultimate expression of the marvelous deeds of God.

Both speeches end with interruptions by the listeners; in Acts 22, the Jews start shouting and causing a disturbance (vv. 22–23), while in Acts 26 it is Festus who exclaims that Paul is mad. The interruptions simply create a dramatic close, for Paul's speech in each case is complete.

The Speeches in Context

The speeches occur in a final section of Acts, where Paul has been arrested, will appear before various authorities, and finally will be sent to Rome under his claim to be heard by the emperor. It is there in Rome that Luke's geographical schema will be complete, as he depicts Paul preaching the gospel to those who will listen.

At the start of this chapter, we noted that the inclusion of three accounts of Paul's conversion signals the great importance this event had for Luke. First, there is the outstanding fact that a former opponent of the Christian movement, who by his own admission persecuted the church "violently" (Gal 1:13), was turned into the foremost missionary preacher among the Gentiles. For any historian of the first century, this momentous change had to be recorded and explained. Luke clearly saw this as God's intervention, not only in an individual life, but also in the life of the church. Second, Luke saw in Paul's experience another version of the Old Testament prophetic call, which confirmed for him the ongoing voice of prophecy in the new movement; it helped to establish the continuity of the Christian church with Israel. He retold the incident through Paul's speeches to develop his thinking about the spread of the gospel to the wider Gentile world.

From the original version, Paul's commissioning has changed. In Acts 9 Paul is apparently told nothing directly of his mission; instead it is through Ananias' vision that we learn God's purpose for Paul. Then, according to Paul's speech in Chapter 22, it was Ananias who informed him of his mission to be a witness to the whole world, but in the temple vision it is Jesus who reveals that Paul is to go to the Gentiles. Now, in this third version of his experience, Paul says that it was on the Damascus road that Jesus commissioned him to go to the Gentiles. As Paul narrates his experience through the speeches, Ananias has a smaller role in Chapter 22, and disappears entirely in Chapter 26 (the same is true of Paul's fellow travelers). Instead, the commissioning by Jesus has become more immediate. From the simple instruction to go into the city in Acts 9:6 and 22:10, the Lord speaking to Paul reveals to him fully his purpose, which is to testify and to go to the Gentiles "to open their eyes" (26:16–18). It is as if Paul has come to a clearer understanding of what his original experience means.

Paul's blindness, too, has undergone a transformation over the three accounts, and is a counterpoint to the theme of light, which itself becomes progressively brighter. In Chapter 9, it is a "light from heaven" that "flashed," causing Paul to fall to the ground (v. 3); according to 22:6, "about noon a great light from heaven suddenly shone" about him; and in 26:13 it was a "light from heaven, brighter than the sun, shining around me and my companions." The appearance at midday of a light brighter than the sun reinforces the brilliance of that light. Conversely, Paul's blindness gradually disappears: At first he is clearly blind, "without sight" for three days (9:9), healed when "something like scales fell from his eyes" (9:18); next, he is simply unable to see because of the brightness of the light (22:11) and is healed by Ananias, almost at once it would seem (22:13—there is no reference to three days); finally, there is no mention at all of Paul's blindness, but rather of the spiritual blindness of the Gentiles. Paul is to "open their eyes so that they may turn from darkness to light," part of the Messiah's intent to "proclaim light" to the Gentiles. Whether or not Paul was factually rendered blind by his experience finally becomes irrelevant: blindness is a metaphor for the inability to see the truth about Jesus.

Speeches in Ancient History Writing

In a modern history, any speech included would be a verbatim report taken from minutes, written records or audio recordings of some kind. Not so in the ancient world, which lacked modern means of preserving someone's words. Yet speeches were considered an indispensable component of Greek and Roman histories, accounting for about 20–35 percent of the total work. In Acts the proportion of speeches is high, about 30 percent, and thus demonstrates the importance they had for Luke. Most scholars point to Hellenistic histories[1] as comparable models for Luke's work, but the historical works of the Hebrew Bible also contain major speeches.

Historians thought it essential to provide speeches for their major personages. According to ancient standards, speeches should consist of what a person said or would most likely have said in the circumstances. Some writers created speeches freely but others were opposed to such invention. Even Thucydides, generally considered to be the founder of objective history writing, admitted to creative interpretation of what his historical characters said. The principle was to recreate as nearly as possible what was most apt for the situation. Luke probably had the classical model to call on, but he also had the example of the Old Testament, in his case the Greek translation of the Hebrew Bible (the Septuagint). There we find significant speeches in the mouths of key figures, most particularly Moses: The Book of Deuteronomy is organized as the speech of Moses to the Israelites in the wilderness (see Deut 1:1–5; 5:1; 31:1), with a few narrative sections. Speeches of various kinds occur also in the historical books, and especially in the Deuterocanonical books of the Maccabees, to which we shall turn later.

1. The term *Hellenistic* refers to the form and style of Greek found across the eastern half of the Roman Empire. See also the following chapters.

In Acts, key speeches are found in the mouths of Peter and Paul, as Luke's two major figures, but also in the mouths of others such as Stephen (Chapter 7) and James (15:13–21). Luke follows the usual characteristics of ancient speeches, using typical rhetorical style and adapting the speech to its audience, but the content reveals Luke's theology and probably also reflects the preaching of the early church. Through the speech, Luke interprets the events he is narrating. There is a certain structure to the speeches addressed to those outside the community. The speaker begins with an appeal for a hearing (for example, Acts 2:14; 7:2; 13:16; 22:1; 26:2–3); often there is a history or background (Paul's recital of his education and former life, for example), before the main point of Christian belief is expounded. An interruption may appear to end the speech, but in fact it is already complete; the interruption is a literary device.

As we saw in Acts 15, there are two speeches by Peter and James that are decisive for questions concerning Gentiles. Following the conversion of Cornelius in Chapter 10, Peter is able to say that he is the one "through whom the Gentiles would hear the message of the good news and become believers" (15:6). Peter represents the apostolic leadership, who would have had to agree to this move. Luke, aware of the spread of the gospel among the Gentiles, is in effect confirming that the inclusion of Gentiles was a church decision (11:1–18), as was the decision not to require strict observance of Jewish ritual. It is through Peter's words that the position of the early church is expressed. Note that the speech comes after the debate (15:17), so that Peter's speech has the effect of summing up, closing debate, and finalizing the decision. Similarly, the speech of James, which turns to another topic, expresses a decision made later to require food and marriage restrictions of the non-Jews in the church.[2] In Luke's history, James acts as the spokesman for the Jerusalem church, confirmed by Paul's comments in Galatians (2:12). Peter and James are provided with speeches that faithfully reflect the position of the church on these issues, which is how speeches work in ancient histories.

---

2. See Chapter 2 above.

Paul's speeches, too, not only address his own situation but point beyond, to an interpretation of his experience in the life of the church. In Acts 22, Paul is at great pains to assert his Jewishness; Luke's theology is that belief in Jesus is a continuation of Jewish belief, not a contradiction to it. (Luke also, however, paints a picture of Jews who stubbornly refuse to believe, who are hostile to the Christian message, and who are finally excluded from it, to the benefit of the Gentiles: Acts 28:23–28.) In Acts 26, Paul's speech reveals how powerful is the work of God, transforming him into a believer, but more powerfully still raising the dead, of whom the Messiah is the first (v. 23). Paul is a living example of the salvation of God, which is open to all and which forgives sins of those who repent.

Thus, in Acts, Paul's conversion is not simply an account of a vision and a change of heart and action. Through the dramatization of the event, and Paul's recounting of it in speech form, Luke is able to present and illustrate key ideas of his theology, to provide a history of early Christianity which confirms faith.

For Further Reading

Richard Baukham, "Kerygmatic Summaries in the Speeches of Acts" in Ben Witherington, III, ed., *History, Literature, and Society in the Book of Acts* (Cambridge: Cambridge University Press, 1996), pp. 185–217.

Carolyn Osiek, "Characters: The Spice of the Story," *The Bible Today* (September 1999), 276–280.

For Further Study

1. Read Peter's speeches in Acts 2:14–36 and 3:12–26. Compare them for content and style. What do these speeches reveal about Luke's understanding of the Christian message?

2. Read the speeches of Paul in Acts 13:16–43 and 17:22–31. Note the immediate context: Where does each speech take place and to whom? How does this affect the style of Paul's address and the content of the speech?

3. Read the "Last Discourse" of Jesus in John 13–16. How would the understanding of this passage be affected by seeing it as a speech like those in Acts?

6

THE BOOKS OF MACCABEES
IN CONTEXT

In this section we turn to the books of Maccabees, probably not very familiar to most readers. They are found in the Catholic and Orthodox scriptures but not in the Protestant Old Testament, which follows the Hebrew (Jewish) Bible.[1] Although not regarded as Jewish scripture, these books are important for Jewish history since they relate significant events in the life of Judea and Judaism. There are actually four books bearing the title Maccabees but we are concerned only with the first two. The books of 1 and 2 Maccabees, which relate two versions of the Maccabean rebellion in the second century B.C.E., were written by different authors with alternative viewpoints. For our purposes this is an advantage, since we can read one against the other to get a clearer picture of each author's unique style. In the next three chapters, we shall explore some passages from both books for further insight into the composition of biblical history. Before reading specific texts, however, we shall review the historical, cultural, and literary contexts.

The Historical Context:
The Second Temple Period

In order to understand the issues contained in the books of Maccabees, we must look at the wider picture of the political realities of the day. In the second century B.C.E., the inhabitants of Judea

---

1. Some Protestant editions of the Bible will include the Apocrypha, where the books of Maccabees can be found.

were living under Seleucid rule in the hellenizing world of the eastern Mediterranean. This simple statement is filled with political and cultural assumptions, which need to be unpacked.

The end of the old kingdom of Judah came with the fall of Jerusalem to the Babylonian Empire in 587 B.C.E. and the subsequent exile of some of the population to Babylon. With the last king under house arrest in the Babylonian court, the monarchy came to an end. Yet before too long another empire arose to challenge and defeat the Babylonians in 539 B.C.E.—the Persians under Cyrus, whose policy was to permit exiled groups to return to their own lands. Among these were the Judeans, many of whom as a result regarded Cyrus as God's envoy.[2] The returning Judeans rebuilt Jerusalem and the temple, although the area remained but a minor province in the Persian Empire.

This stage of Judea's history is referred to as the Second Temple period, a time of restoration and of clarifying the religious tradition, a time when revered writings were being re-edited and collected as a body of scripture. It was also a time when many Judeans, as a result of the events surrounding the exile, had either remained in Babylonia or had migrated to other lands, forming new communities while maintaining their old traditions.

A major political and cultural shift took place when the young and dynamic Alexander the Great appeared on the scene (336–323 B.C.E.). Inheriting the throne of Macedonia when his father Philip was assassinated, Alexander set about expanding his father's dominions from Greece into the empires of the East. This he managed with remarkable success, taking over one region after another until he reached as far as the Indus River. He then turned back towards Egypt, bringing that empire also under his control. Alexander's goal, however, was not simply military; it was also cultural. He established colonies (usually named after himself) along his route in a conscious attempt to further Greek civilization. It has been suggested that Alexander's admiration for all things Greek came from the influence

---

2. 2 Chron 36:22–23; Ezra 1:1; see also Isa 41:2–4, where the "victor from the east" is Cyrus.

of his childhood tutor, the philosopher Aristotle. Greek was to be the language of government, of trade and commerce, and of education. The empire was to be unified by a common culture and values, and although Alexander died young and his empire divided among ambitious generals, his legacy of hellenization remained. Through his efforts and the continuation of his policies by his successors, the eastern Mediterranean became Greek and stayed Greek.

Two rival kingdoms ultimately emerged from the division of Alexander's empire, ruled by dynasties stemming from two of his successors, Ptolemy and Seleucus. The Ptolemies controlled Egypt, the Seleucids ruled an area from modern Turkey to modern Iran and Iraq—the area that had been controlled successively by Assyria, Babylonia, and Persia. The two superpowers continued the age-old struggle for dominance in the region, pushing against each other in the Levant and Palestine.[3] Judea was again caught in the middle, under the control of one, then the other. The same instability in the region, however, also allowed small kingdoms to establish themselves. In this context the time was ripe for the subprovince of Judea to assert itself under the Maccabees (a family more properly known as the Hasmoneans) as an independent entity and later as a small kingdom. But at the time of the events narrated in Maccabees, Judea was ruled by the Seleucids in the person of Antiochus IV Epiphanes.

The Cultural Context: Hellenization

The term *Hellenism* is used to express the effects of Alexander's move to spread the benefits of Greek culture throughout his empire. From *hellene,* meaning "Greek," hellenization refers to the assimilation (in varying degrees) of Greek language and culture by the lands under the control of Alexander and his successors. The result of the interaction between indigenous cultures and Greek was the Hellenistic world. It would seem that the upper classes in more

---

3. "Palestine" derives from "Philistine" and was the name in the Greek period for the region extending roughly from Lebanon to Sinai and from the Mediterranean coast to the desert area of Transjordan.

urban areas became more readily hellenized as they were more likely to benefit from the new regimes. With the Greek language came Greek ideas and values, education, Greek models for society, for the city, for the body politic. Trade and commerce adopted Greek standards and terminology. The gods, too, quite easily adopted the names of their Greek counterparts. Not only did Greek become the common language of the educated classes, Greek vocabulary seeped into the native languages as well. All levels of society were ultimately affected by the cultural shift of hellenization.

The effects of Alexander's policy of hellenization created a Greek-speaking world imbued with Greek concepts and thinking that would last for centuries. Much later, this would be the world of the first Christians, who consequently would write their letters, gospels, and histories in the Hellenistic Greek of the eastern Mediterranean. Greek terminology would express early Christian theology: baptism, eucharist, apostle, presbyter, deacon, even the title Christ, all these words come directly from Greek into Christian vocabulary. The eastern half of the Roman Empire (known as the Byzantine Empire from the fifth century C.E.) would remain Greek when the rest of the empire became Latin. In Christian history, the distant effects of hellenization of the eastern Mediterranean can still be seen today in the ancient liturgies of some of the eastern Christian churches. Throughout the political changes in this part of the world, the cultural effects of Alexander's empire would continue.

In this hellenized world lived the Judeans—in Persia (the former Babylon), in Egypt, in such Greek cities as Sparta, Delos, and Rhodes, and elsewhere. Palestine itself with an influx of Greek garrisons was not immune to hellenization. Cities organized on the Greek model were established in places such as Ptolemais (Acre) and Askelon on the coast, Scythopolis (Beth Shean) in the Jordan Valley, and Gadara and Philadelphia (Amman) in Transjordan. Interaction between the *diaspora*[4] and Jerusalem undoubtedly introduced aspects of Hellenism to the homeland. Since many Judeans, or Jews as they

---

4. A Greek word meaning "scattered," designating those Judeans who lived outside the homeland.

are also called, maintained the religious traditions of their ancestors, most notably the worship of their own God, they had to come to terms with the polytheistic world in which they now lived.

A major question was the extent to which Jews could be assimilated into the surrounding culture without losing the essentials of their faith. While their neighbors worshiped various deities, sometimes out of civic duty rather than conviction, Jews worshiped only one God and refused to have any other cultic association. They practiced circumcision, which was thought to be barbaric by Greek standards, and they followed the teachings of certain holy books. By the second century B.C.E., they also observed rituals of purification and ate separately from non-Jews. Some of the writings that emerged in this period reflect the situation of being a Jew in a Gentile world; for example, references to avoiding Gentile food occur in the books of Daniel (1:8), Esther (12:19), and Tobit (1:10–11). Not everyone agreed on the need to stay separate from Gentiles. While many Jews did in fact adopt a Hellenistic lifestyle like that of their neighbors, it did not necessarily mean that they had abandoned their ancestral faith. It did mean that some found ways to be both culturally hellenized and religiously Jewish, less observant of custom than other Jews. Their opponents, who remained adamantly traditional, emerged as a movement of *hasidim* or Hasideans ("faithful" or "pious").[5] It was among such people that the Maccabees first gained support.

The most obvious cultural influence was in language. Besides numerous inscriptions of all kinds, the common use of Greek personal names gives ample evidence of the spread of the language into everyday Jewish life and even into Jerusalem, which was a backwater for much of the time. For instance, at the end of the Greek version of Esther, there is reference to Ptolemy and Lysimachus, father and son of a priestly family of Jerusalem, both with Greek names. (Lysimachus seems to have been the translator of the book.) Even the high priest in Jerusalem could have a Greek name, such as Jason and Menelaus, just prior to the Maccabean revolt. In the books of

---

5. Since the designation *Hasidim* has a modern connotation, I shall use the parallel term "Hasideans" (Greek, *asidaioi*) to refer to this movement of Torah loyalists.

Maccabees, many of the personal names are Greek, even among those who were opposed to hellenization.

The Literary Context

One significant outcome of the cultural shift was the need to translate the sacred writings for those Jews who had lost familiarity with Hebrew. A pious legend tells of seventy-two scribes from Jerusalem being assembled in Alexandria, Egypt, to translate the Torah (the first five books of the Bible) into Greek. Their sacred task was affirmed when it was discovered that each scribe, although isolated from the rest, had produced exactly the same translation! The Greek Bible later came to be known as the Septuagint (from the Latin for seventy) in reference to this miraculous event. The connection with Alexandria is not coincidental. A typical Hellenistic city, Alexandria was also a center of learning, boasting an immense library said to contain a copy of every book ever written. The city remained a leading center of education well into the Christian era until an overzealous emperor had the library burned to rid the world of pagan writings. Alexandria, however, also had a sizable Jewish community, which would make the idea of a Greek translation of scripture readily understandable. The fact that a contemporary audience could easily believe that so many Greek-speaking scribes were available in Jerusalem says much about the extent of hellenization among the diaspora Jews. By the time the Book of Sirach (Ben Sirah) was translated by his grandson in 132 B.C.E., there were already Greek versions of Jewish scriptures. The translator refers to these books and further mentions the difficulty of rendering the original into another language:

> For what was originally expressed in Hebrew does not have exactly the same sense when translated into another language. Not only this book [that is, Sirach], but even the Law itself, the Prophecies, and the rest of the books differ not a little when read in the original. (Prologue)

71

Besides translations of Hebrew or Aramaic originals, some writings composed in Greek, such as the Wisdom of Solomon, became popular and accepted as sacred. Others seem to have been more popular in their Greek versions, since this is the way they have come down to us and their Hebrew originals are lost (for example, the Book of Judith). The Greek version of Esther included additions that, in effect, rewrote the book from a different perspective. Some writings of the period reveal the influence of the Hellenistic novel (for example, Tobit, Esther). Jewish writers also produced histories in the Hellenistic style, among them 1 and 2 Maccabees, which unlike other histories were accepted into the Greek canon as sacred books.

These secondary writings were not universally accepted, however. As Judaism and Christianity defined themselves more clearly and developed separately, each had its own canon (list) of what constituted scripture, or authoritative sacred writings. Both traditions had in common the books of the Hebrew Bible. Because of their preference for the Greek versions, however, Christians also had their "second" list, the deuterocanon that Judaism in the end did not accept as scripture. As Christians added their own specifically Christian writings, the earlier books became the "Old" Testament. Much later, in the Protestant Reformation, the Reformers omitted the books of the deuterocanon, referring to them as "apocrypha." Thus arose the difference between the Catholic and Orthodox Old Testament, on the one hand, and the Protestant, on the other. The books of Maccabees belong to the second list, the deuterocanon.[6]

The Maccabean Rebellion

The events portrayed in 1 and 2 Maccabees took place in the second century B.C.E. in a Judea controlled by the Seleucid dynasty. The main sources for what happened are the books of Maccabees and the Jewish historian Josephus, who wrote late in the first

---

6. Today, scholars of all denominations tend to use the term *deuterocanon.*

century C.E. Corroboration for some of the details comes from other ancient sources.

As we noted earlier, Alexander's empire in the eastern Mediterranean was divided between two rival dynasties, the Ptolemies in Egypt and the Seleucids in what had been the Persian Empire. For about a century, Palestine, including the little province of Judea, had been controlled by the Ptolemies, but in 198 B.C.E., Ptolemy V had been defeated in battle at Paneas[7] by Antiochus III, the then Seleucid king, who thus gained control of Palestine. By 175, the kingdom had passed to his son Antiochus IV Epiphanes. This Antiochus intended to expand his kingdom but also to unify it by an aggressive policy of hellenization, both of which activities required funding.

In Jerusalem, the high priest's brother Jason took advantage of the situation by buying the priestly office from the new king, in 174 B.C.E. Onias, the high priest and a respected leader, was accordingly deposed and Jason took his place to the dismay of many Jews, not only because of the way he achieved the high priesthood but also because he was a hellenizer, no doubt a factor in Antiochus's decision. Antiochus was willing to extend citizenship of Antioch to those who took up the Greek way of life, an offer that Jason applied for on behalf of Jerusalem. He did not enjoy his position for long, however, since in 172 B.C.E. another claimant, Menelaus, bought the high priesthood in his turn, and later had Onias III killed. It was also said that Menelaus used temple money to finance his ambition. The reaction to these moves was violent protest in Jerusalem. Nevertheless, under both high priests the hellenization of Jerusalem went forward.

In 169 B.C.E., Antiochus returning from a campaign against Egypt detoured to Jerusalem and the temple treasury to replenish his resources, with the compliance of Menelaus. Again there were angry protests, which Antiochus put down harshly. In 167, he stationed a garrison of Syrian troops in Jerusalem and followed this with further repressive measures, including a ban on certain Jewish religious

---

7. Paneas or Banias was known as Caesarea Philippi in the first century C.E.

practices, such as circumcision, observing the Sabbath, and keeping religious festivals. At this point, Antiochus also brought pagan worship into the temple, setting up "the abomination of abominations" (probably a statue of Zeus) in the sacred precincts. The people of Jerusalem and Judea were now expected to follow the official Seleucid cult in their own sacred precincts.

These actions were unprecedented in the ancient world, which was open to a diversity of religious beliefs and traditions. Rulers were generally tolerant of local customs and made no effort to interfere. Probably it was the king's aggressive policy of hellenization and his reaction to the various protests that led him to impose a uniformity of religious practice, banning local observances and promoting the worship of Zeus. Elsewhere, people had quite readily adopted Greek names for local gods and had adopted Seleucid cultic practices, so perhaps Antiochus thought the Jews would do likewise with their God. If this was the case, it backfired dramatically. Jewish reaction took several forms. There were those among the hellenizers who supported the reforms of Antiochus to a greater or lesser degree, but many were opposed. Some Jews believed that their world was at an end and that only direct and powerful intervention from heaven could avert total destruction. They believed that God had to act— there was no other choice. From this thinking apocalyptic literature began to appear (for example, Daniel 7–12, composed about this time). Other Jews fled to the wilderness areas, to escape the restrictions imposed on them, among them many Hasideans, the Torah loyalists. Still others, however, took up armed resistance.

Among the latter was the priest Mattathias of Modein, who with his sons rallied together many of the disaffected. But it was his son, Judas Maccabeus, or Maccabee, who was remembered as the outstanding leader of the revolt after his father's death in 166 B.C.E., and it was his name that became attached to all the brothers.[8] Waging guerrilla warfare, Judas made important gains against the forces of Antiochus. As the king was already waging war to the east, he sent his regent Lysias to deal with the rebellious Judeans, but in

---

8. "Maccabee" possibly means something like "hammer."

the face of the rebels' successes, Lysias was forced to return to Antioch. Within two years Judas had gained control of Jerusalem, where he reconsecrated the temple in December 164; from that time the Jews celebrated an annual festival of the Dedication,[9] today known as Hanukkah. The Maccabean cause continued to grow in popular support.

In the meantime, Antiochus had died and the regent Lysias continued the war on behalf of the new king Demetrius, still a minor. Just as Lysias began to make headway against Judas and his followers, political problems necessitated his return to Antioch. To settle affairs in Judea, he made a treaty in 162 B.C.E. rescinding the ban on Jewish practices. A new high priest, Alcimus, was appointed who had the support of both Hellenists and some of the Hasideans who thought they would fare better under his leadership. The Maccabees refused to compromise. Hostilities continued. When Nicanor, a Syrian general, was sent from Antioch against Judas, he was defeated so thoroughly that a new festival day was proclaimed, the "day of Nicanor." Yet victory was not to last as Nicanor's replacement not only defeated the Judeans but killed Judas as well (160 B.C.E.).

After this, the Hasmoneans (as the Maccabees are more properly known) and their supporters fled Jerusalem. Judas's brother Jonathan took up the leadership during these years, keeping the struggle alive, until internal Seleucid politics turned the tide. The young king Demetrius was challenged for power by Alexander Balas, both sides trying to gain Jonathan's support with offers of high office. While Jonathan ostensibly supported Alexander, who made him governor of Judea as well as high priest, he continued to play one side against the other, which proved his undoing. He was captured in 143 and was later executed, to be succeeded by yet another Hasmonean brother, Simon. In 142 B.C.E., Simon gave his support to Demetrius in return for a measure of independence for Judea and his own position as high priest as well as governor, which offices he kept until his own death in 134. The Hasmoneans were recognized by the Judeans as legitimate rulers, and their dynasty continued to govern until

---

9. See John 10:22.

direct Roman rule in 63 B.C.E. ended Judea's brief moment of independence. Even then, the Hasmoneans remained as client rulers under the Romans until the time of Herod the Great (37–4 B.C.E.), who astutely married into the family.

This period was the matrix out of which came the sectarianism of the first century. Sadducees, Pharisees, Essenes, and Zealots[10] had their origins in the struggle to interpret the Torah in the Hellenistic world. The Pharisees (whose name probably means *separatist*) seem to have emerged from the Hasideans, who opposed hellenization, avoided Gentile foods, and kept the Sabbath to the point of refusing to defend themselves (1 Macc 1:62; 2:34–38). The Pharisees also believed in resurrection, a belief that appears in 2 Maccabees. The Sadducees apparently saw themselves as the descendants of the priestly house of Zadok (see 2 Sam 15:24–29; 1 Kgs 1:32, 39), having authority and responsibility in temple affairs. As members of the upper class, they were more open to hellenization than the Hasideans. The Essenes, however, disputed the Sadducees' claim to the house of Zadok since the time that the Hasmoneans had taken over the high priesthood. Ironically, the later Hasmoneans had become allied to the Seleucids, and became as hellenizing as any. The "Wicked Priest" mentioned in the Qumran (Dead Sea) documents may even refer to Simon who accepted the office of high priest from Demetrius. The Zealots, who were responsible for several rebellions in the Roman period, combined religious zeal and nationalism, not unlike the Maccabees.

1 and 2 Maccabees

The Maccabees were the warrior heroes who founded the Hasmonean dynasty in Judea in the second century B.C.E. Sometime after the rebellion and the establishment of an independent nation, two histories were written independently of one another to narrate

---

10. All but the Essenes are mentioned in the Christian New Testament.

events and explain why Judea was finally free. Each history had its own interpretation of what had happened, one seeing the rebellion as the beginning of the rise of a powerful dynasty, the other seeing the liberation of Jerusalem and the temple as God's saving intervention on behalf of the holy place. Thus 1 Maccabees follows the history of the entire family through to the death of the youngest brother, Simon, but 2 Maccabees concentrates on the exploits of Judas Maccabeus only. The scope of each history is related also to its purpose and style, which we shall explore in the next two chapters. By way of appropriate excerpts, we shall discover more about ancient history writing, about the kinds of material the authors used and how they used them.

For Further Reading

Any comprehensive history of Israel will include a chapter on the Hellenistic period and the Maccabean revolt and will provide more detail than offered here. Other helpful resources include the following:

Shaye Cohen, *From the Maccabees to the Mishnah* (Philadelphia: Fortress Press, 1987), especially Chapter 2, "Jews and Gentiles," which discusses Hellenism and hellenizing in relationship to Judaism.

Robert B. Coote and Mary P. Coote, *Power, Politics, and the Making of the Bible* (Minneapolis: Fortress Press, 1990), Chapter 12, "Greek Rulers and Rome's Hasmoneans."

J. Andrew Dearman, *Religion and Culture in Ancient Israel* (Peabody, MA: Hendrickson, 1992), especially pp. 114–122.

Lee I. Levine, "The Age of Hellenism: Alexander the Great and the Rise and Fall of the Hasmonean Kingdom" in *Ancient Israel*, rev. and exp. ed., Herschel Shanks, ed. (Upper Saddle River, NJ: Prentice Hall/Biblical Archaeology Society, 1999), pp. 231–264; a good and up-to-date survey of the period.

Morton Smith, *Palestinian Parties and Politics That Shaped the Old Testament* (London: SCM Press, 1987). See Chapter 7, "From Nehemiah to Antiochus Epiphanes," for background to the Hasmonean period.

Michael Stone, *Scriptures, Sects, and Visions* (Philadelphia: Fortress Press, 1980). Although this book deals mainly with a later period (the first centuries B.C.E. and C.E.), Chapter 9 gives an idea of the complexity of Jewish Hellenism.

For Further Study:

Explore the role of Hellenism in the ancient eastern Mediterranean, especially its impact on early Judaism and/or Christianity.

7

WHAT LED TO THE MACCABEAN REVOLT? TWO DIFFERENT VIEWS

The First and Second Books of Maccabees offer alternative perspectives of the same pivotal event: the incursions of Antiochus IV into the temple and the subsequent revolt. While 1 Maccabees is concerned with the Maccabean rebellion in the larger context of the rise of the Hasmoneans in the Hellenistic world, 2 Maccabees focuses on the restoration of the temple and Judas Maccabeus as the hero. The difference in scope is related to the difference in perspective, as we shall discover in the next two chapters. How a history narrates events is as important as what it narrates. We begin with the scope and purpose of each book.

The Introductions

Any historian has to decide where to start, what to put in and what to leave out from the material available, and what will be emphasized or highlighted. A simple list of events is not history; a history attempts to uncover cause and effect, to analyze what happened and why. Moreover, the historian's position will consciously or unconsciously influence the analysis, so no history is unbiased. The interesting question will then be, what is the historian's perspective? How does the historian make his or her point?[1] Ancient historians were not shy about their motivation or goals. For them, good history writing required

---

1. Given that the known ancient historians are male and that the culture of the time and place would scarcely have allowed a female historian, I refer to the authors of 1 and 2 Maccabees as male throughout.

not only good information, but a satisfying arrangement of material, and a didactic purpose. A good history aimed to please as well as educate.

Introductions give us direction. Modern writings often provide a suitably titled section wherein the purpose and scope of the work are indicated. Ancient authors, too, give similar indications either by a clear prologue to the work, or by the order of the contents. Because we shall be reading only extracts from the two books of Maccabees, it is important to read beyond the passages presented here—optimally, the whole book, but at least the chapters surrounding our extracts. As we read the opening section of each book, consider the following questions: Where does the author begin and why? What is included? What is the attitude towards the persons in the narrative? What sort of language is used? What order is followed?

Introduction and the Causes of the Revolt (1)

1 Macc 1:1–10

1. When Alexander son of Philip, the Macedonian, who came from the land of Kittim, had defeated King Darius of the Persians and the Medes, he succeeded him as king. (He had previously become king of Greece.) 2. He fought many battles, conquered strongholds, and put to death the kings of the earth. 3. He advanced to the ends of the earth, and plundered many nations. When the earth became quiet before him, he was exalted, and his heart was lifted up. 4. He gathered a very strong army and ruled over countries, nations, and princes, and they became tributary to him. 5. After this he fell sick and perceived that he was dying. 6. So he summoned his most honored officers, who had been brought up with him from youth, and divided his kingdom among them while he was still alive. 7. And after Alexander had reigned twelve years, he died.

8. Then his officers began to rule, each in his own place. 9. They all put on crowns after his death, and so did their descendants after them for many years; and they caused

many evils on the earth. 10. From them came forth a sinful root, Antiochus Epiphanes, son of King Antiochus; he had been a hostage in Rome. He began to reign in the one hundred thirty-seventh year of the kingdom of the Greeks.

The first thing we notice is that the historian takes us back to Alexander the Great, giving us a very brief summary of his conquests (vv. 1–4). The succession of power from Alexander to his generals is even more summarily dealt with (v. 6; as the notes in my Bible dryly comment, "A complex history of power struggles lies behind this statement"). But the broad sweep across centuries allows the author to reach almost at once the focus of interest, Antiochus, while at the same time sketching the connecting link between Antiochus and Alexander. In other words, although Antiochus is our main concern, the roots go back to Alexander. Only after this does the author turn to specifics, events that happened "in those days," that is, in the time of Antiochus.

Why would the author start here? Two reasons are suggested: first, because the conflict in the ensuing history turns on the hellenizing effects of Alexander's empire, and second, because the author wants to place the history on the world stage. This is a history of a self-determined nation within an international context. It is the story of "how we arrived" at nationhood. The scope of the history is also indicated by the use of an international dating system, as we see in v. 10; thus, our story begins with the accession of Antiochus "in the one hundred thirty-seventh year of the kingdom of the Greeks" (v. 10).[2]

If you have read through 1 Macc 1, you will have noticed that the account proceeds in a straightforward way. The author tells us what Antiochus did in Jerusalem and in what context (after his campaign against Egypt). The author also provides a chronology giving us

---

2. Luke's Gospel similarly sets the story of Jesus in the context of world events, dating events not simply by local rulers "during the high priesthood of Annas and Caiaphas" but very specifically "in the fifteenth year of the reign of the Emperor Tiberius" (Luke 3:1–2).

dates as we would expect in a history (vv. 10, 20, 29, 54), and in fact continues to provide dates throughout the book (see also 2:70; 3:37; 4:52, etc.). Both 1 and 2 Maccabees use "the Greek era," which was the standard dating system for the Seleucid kingdom and begins with the first year of Seleucus I in 312 B.C.E. But the new year could begin in either fall or spring, depending on whether the writer's source was using the official Syrian practice or Babylonian practice. The Syrian usage is generally followed in 1 Maccabees (with some exceptions), and the Babylonian in 2 Maccabees. Although there are some problems with the author's accuracy, it is clear from the careful use of dates throughout that the author has a historical intent to produce a chronological account of what happened.

Because the historian has started with Alexander, we can now see an association between Antiochus and the Greek king. Alexander is the ultimate cause of all the problems in Judea, since it was his conquests which brought the region under the control of the Seleucids, and his policy of hellenization which had affected the Jewish way of life. Alexander's successors "caused many evils on the earth" (v. 9), which must refer at least to the wars between Egypt and Syria but could also refer to the effects of hellenization. Antiochus is himself called "a sinful root," which immediately tells us on which side of the fence this historian sits.

But notice what happens next in the text. Immediately after the announcement of Antiochus's reign (v. 10), and before going on to relate what he did (v. 16), something else is added.

1 Macc 1:11–15

11. In those days certain renegades came out from Israel and misled many, saying, "Let us go and make a covenant with the Gentiles around us, for since we separated from them many disasters have come upon us." 12. This proposal pleased them, 13. and some of the people eagerly went to the king, who authorized them to observe the ordinances of the Gentiles. 14. So they built a gymnasium in Jerusalem, according to the Gentile custom, 15. and

removed the marks of circumcision, and abandoned the holy covenant. They joined with the Gentiles and sold themselves to do evil.

Of course we recognize here the reference to the hellenization that went on in Jerusalem, specifically to the actions of Jason the high priest. And the author is not unbiased; the hellenizers are called "renegades" (literally, "lawless men") and are said to have "sold themselves to do evil."

Behind this passage is the reality of differences among Jews over the extent to which one could adopt Greek lifestyle, particularly with its political and social advantages, while still remaining faithful to the religion of the ancestors. Those who believed one should remain separated from Gentiles obviously opposed, sometimes vehemently, those who were hellenized to a greater or lesser degree. Thus our author, on the side of the purists, refers consistently to hellenized Jews as "renegades" throughout the history.

You may have noticed that the renegades are said to have come from "Israel." This is clearly not a reference to the ancient northern kingdom, for this passage is concerned with Jerusalem. Rather, *Israel* here refers to the religious tradition, what today we should call Judaism; the term *Judaism* does not appear in the relevant literature until 2 Maccabees, and then remains rare.[3] *Israel* is the usual biblical term for the religion of the Judeans, in the Second Temple period. The Greek word *ioudaioi* (Judeans), which is usually translated as *Jews,* is primarily the designation of the inhabitants of Judea, although it can also refer to their religious allegiance.[4]

By way of introduction, the writer has arranged the material beautifully to provide the context, but also to identify the causes of what will be narrated just a little further on. Alexander is the distant cause because of the results of his conquests, and Antiochus, the "sinful root," is the near cause; his actions will be detailed. Before

---

3. In the New Testament, only Paul uses the term "Judaism"—once, in Gal 1:14.
4. It follows that any occurrence of the designation "Jews" in biblical texts must be checked to discover whether the reference is religious or political.

that, however, another group is introduced—the "renegades." They, too, are to blame for what happened because of their eagerness to grasp Gentile ways and to "abandon the holy covenant." All that follows can be traced back to these causes. In a few short verses, the author has established both context and atmosphere. From here on, events will be described in more detail.

A brief survey of 1 Maccabees 1–2 shows that the author moves quickly to the actions of Antiochus and, after a summary of the Egyptian campaign, relates how Antiochus made an incursion into Jerusalem to plunder the temple treasury. Later, Antiochus instituted his policy of uniformity of religious practice, persecuting those who would not comply. In response, those who remained faithful to the laws of Israel either died passively (1:62–63) or joined the uprising led by Mattathias and his sons (2:1–48). The history then follows the career of Judas and his brothers up to the death of Simon, and the accession of his son Jonathan.

Introduction and the Cause of the Revolt (2)

The alternative history in 2 Maccabees begins with two chapters of introduction (2 Macc 1:1–2:32), which may seem like too much of a good thing. But again, the arrangement of material has a purpose. The text we begin with here is usually termed the author's preface, although it is preceded by two letters, but more about that later. As you read, keep in mind how 1 Maccabees began and also pay attention to the wording. What is important for this writer and why?

2 Macc 2:19–23

19. The story of Judas Maccabeus and his brothers, and the purification of the great temple, and the dedication of the altar, 20. and further the wars against Antiochus Epiphanes and his son Eupator, 21. and the appearances that came from heaven to those who fought bravely for Judaism, so that though few in number they seized the

whole land and pursued the barbarian hordes, 22. and regained the possession of the temple famous throughout the world, and liberated the city, and re-established the laws that were about to be abolished, while the Lord with great kindness became gracious to them—23. all this, which has been set forth by Jason of Cyrene in five volumes, we shall attempt to condense into a single book.

There is no doubt about the aim of this book: It is a condensed version, usually designated the "epitome," of an already existing but lengthy work by a certain Jason of Cyrene.[5] Nor is there any doubt about the contents, which are summarized very quickly in this preface. The book concludes with the victory of Judas over Nicanor, and the general rejoicing that resulted (15:28–36), followed by the epitomist's note "Here I will end my story." Notice, however, what has priority for the author: This is the "story of Judas Maccabeus and his brothers, *and the purification of the great temple, and the dedication of the altar.*" The wars against Antiochus are secondary. What else is the author concerned with? The preface notes that Judas was also responsible for re-establishing the laws that were about to be abolished, namely the laws of Torah. Nor is the writer shy about attributing divine graciousness to the Maccabees, including visions from heaven. So, in summarizing the content of the earlier history, the emphasis is clearly on Judas and his religious achievements, brought about almost coincidentally by his military activity.

Later, we shall return to these themes of 2 Maccabees, but for the moment we shall concentrate on the author's preface, which continues as follows:

2 Macc 2:24–32

24. For considering the flood of statistics involved and the difficulty there is for those who wish to enter upon the narratives of history because of the mass of material, 25. we

5. Unfortunately, nothing more is known about this early Jewish historian.

have aimed to please those who wish to read, to make it easy for those who are inclined to memorize, and to profit all readers. 26. For us who have undertaken the toil of abbreviating, it is no light matter but calls for sweat and loss of sleep, 27. just as it is not easy for one who prepares a banquet and seeks the benefit of others. Nevertheless, to secure the gratitude of many we will gladly endure the uncomfortable toil, 28. leaving the responsibility for exact details to the compiler, while devoting our effort to arriving at the outlines of the condensation. 29. For as the master builder of a new house must be concerned with the whole construction, while the one who undertakes its painting and decoration has to consider only what is suitable for its adornment, such in my judgment is the case with us. 30. It is the duty of the original historian to occupy the ground, to discuss matters from every side, and to take trouble with details, 31. but the one who recasts the narrative should be allowed to strive for brevity of expression and to forego exhaustive treatment. 32. At this point therefore let us begin our narrative, without adding any more to what has already been said; for it would be foolish to lengthen the preface while cutting short the history itself.

If nothing else, this author has a sense of humor! Besides the last comment, I think the remarks about sweat and loss of sleep are a little tongue-in-cheek. It seems to me that if we read the whole passage from this perspective, we find a light touch, a little self-deprecation, on the part of the writer. In fact, the stated purpose of the abridgement is to be pleasing and to make it a little easier for the reader. It was a respected aim for ancient authors, to make a serious work both instructive and entertaining, as we see in v. 25. The epitomist compares himself to one who prepares a banquet for the pleasure of others, but also to an interior decorator (v. 29), not so much concerned with the major structures as with beautifying the individual rooms. Again, at the end of the book, the writer compares the finished work to a judicious mixture of wine and water, which is delicious and enjoyable (15:39). In doing so, the writer tells us what to expect—and what not to expect. We should not expect to find a lengthy, detailed narrative ("exhaustive treatment," v. 31), nor even to find a balanced account (v. 30); that is the job of the serious or professional historian. Rather, the epitomist who condenses the narrative is allowed more flexibility in the pursuit of a shorter, more accessible version which the general reader would be more likely to enjoy.

Both the preface and the conclusion bring in a personal note, which is quite unusual in biblical books, although the prologue to the Greek translation of Sirach, written by Sirach's grandson, also injects a personal note about the difficulties of translating. Since the Greek translation and 2 Maccabees belong roughly to the same era, it is not entirely surprising to find such similarities. Then too we can look forward (chronologically) to Luke's Gospel and Acts, which also have personalized introductions. In fact, the inclusion of a personal preface is typical of Greek style.

At the same time, we also get a glimpse at reading practices of the ancient world, which the writer mentions in a very matter-of-fact way. The very last verse of 2 Maccabees says that "the style of the story delights the *ears* of those who read the work." In the ancient world, and indeed continuing well into the Middles Ages, people were accustomed to read aloud even in private; silent reading was virtually unknown. (This can make a difference with some texts, especially poetic texts, whose pattern may be more discernible to the ear than to the eye.) Secondly, in the preface, the epitomist refers to those who wish to memorize what they read or hear (2:25). Very few individuals had their own copies of written works since they were copied by hand, a lengthy task and therefore very expensive. Manuscript copies were borrowed and thus circulated, so it would be an advantage to memorize what one had read while the copy was available. Afterwards, the reader would quote from memory. This can be seen in some New Testament texts, where the writer has apparently quoted from memory, but not quite accurately. See, for instance, Mark 1:2–3, where the first part of the "quotation from

Isaiah" is actually from Malachi 3:1. Matthew's Gospel, however, gets it right (3:3).[6] It pays to be alert to these details that, while not essential to understanding the passage in question, nonetheless shed a little light on the ancient world from which the text comes.

What sort of a historian is the author of 2 Maccabees? The author's purpose is to provide a historical account of the desecration and purification of the temple. It may be limited in scope, but it is still a history. The epitomist eschews the role of professional historian and seems to be rather what we would today call a popularizer, someone who makes the heavy material of serious scholarship more accessible to the general reader.

2 Macc 3:1–4:50

As we saw in 1 Maccabees, the immediate cause of the Maccabean rebellion was the incursion of Antiochus IV into Jerusalem on his return from his Egyptian campaign, his looting of the temple treasury and the later prohibitions of Jewish religious practices. A reasonably accurate account of all this is given in 1 Maccabees immediately following the introductory background (1:16–63). The story of Mattathias ensues (2:1–48). In 2 Maccabees, however, Antiochus and his Egyptian campaign are not mentioned until Chapter 5; the history begins with the high priest Onias. This is not simply background to the exploits of Judas but reflects the overall purpose of the history, which is not to relate the political independence of Judea.

2 Macc 3:1–3

1. While the holy city was inhabited in unbroken peace and the laws were strictly observed because of the piety of the high priest Onias and his hatred of wickedness, 2. it came about that the kings themselves honored the

---

6. Other discrepancies between quotations in the New Testament and their Old Testament sources may originate from the LXX (Septuagint) version.

place and glorified the temple with the finest presents, 3. even to the extent that King Seleucus of Asia defrayed from his own revenues all the expenses connected with the service of the sacrifices.

The language is revealing. Jerusalem, not yet named (except in the address of the preceding letters), is simply "the holy city," said to have experienced "unbroken peace." These words indicate the mind of the writer, thinking of Jerusalem as the center of religious activity rather than as a political entity, and looking back (through rose-colored lenses) to a golden era of peace, at least from the perspective of the later history of repression and rebellion. "The laws were strictly observed" refers to the observance of Torah law, given that the piety of the high priest is instrumental in this state of affairs. Onias is clearly a model high priest. The temple is the focus of the whole chapter, which is hardly surprising in a history dedicated to the account of the desecration of the temple by Antiochus and its restoration by the hero Judas Maccabeus. The history continues in 2 Macc 3 with the story of an attempt to plunder the temple treasury. It is an emotionally charged account, detailing the distress and anxiety of people and priests. The treasury, and therefore the temple's integrity, is saved at the last minute by divine intervention. The whole story leaves no doubt of the temple's sanctity and importance for the faithful; any attempt to violate the holy place will be met with divine retribution.[7]

Next, 2 Macc 4 narrates the actions of Jason, the corrupt high priest, who bought his office from the new king, Antiochus. Here, the focus is on the effects of Jason's leadership on the temple priests, who "were no longer intent upon their service at the altar"; they despised the sanctuary and neglected the sacrifices (v. 14). Again divine retribution is exacted for neglect of the sacred laws.

For this reason heavy disaster overtook them, and those whose ways of living they admired and wished to imitate completely became their enemies and punished them. It

---

7. We shall take a closer look at this section in the next chapter.

is no light thing to show irreverence to the divine laws—
a fact that later events will make clear. (vv. 16–17)

When Antiochus does finally enter the temple, desecrating it
and plundering the treasury (5:15–20), divine retribution is anticipated (v. 20) and not found lacking. Later in the history, Antiochus
was struck by a dreadful illness which eventually brought him to
acknowledge God and his own arrogance (9:1–12).

In the summarized history, the epitomist has chosen a temple-
related incident to begin the sequence of events. More significantly, it
is the malfeasance of Simon, the temple administrator (3:4), who
betrays the trust of the temple. According to the history, the Syrians are
for the moment misinformed, rather than inherently evil. It is internal
politics that nearly causes the desecration of the temple at that point.
Similarly, it is Jason who, having removed the pious high priest Onias
from office, leads the people away from the faithful observance of the
law. Second Maccabees lays the responsibility for disaster on the heads
of faithless Jews, in contrast to First Maccabees, which puts the onus
instead on the hellenizing policies of Alexander and Antiochus, albeit
supported by some "renegades" of Israel. The whole is dictated by the
underlying theology, which fits well with that of the Hasideans.

The choice of where to start the respective histories is already
dictated by the point each wants to make. 1 Maccabees begins with
Alexander and the effects of his conquests, while 2 Maccabees
traces the root causes to an unworthy temple priesthood and neglect
of the law. The first history will highlight the need to counter the
Seleucid Empire militarily, the second will show how observance of
the law leads to restoration of the temple's rightful place. While both
histories are concerned with events surrounding the Maccabean
revolt, their analysis of the problem and the solution differs.

The Use of Documents in History Writing

As it stands now, 2 Maccabees is prefaced by two letters (1:1–9
and 1:10–2:18), both of them from the Jews of Jerusalem to the Jews

in Egypt (probably in Alexandria, where there was a large Jewish community), and both encouraging the celebration of the dedication of the temple (1:9;⁸ 2:16). Standing at the head of the narrative, they create a certain tone: The story of the purification of the temple can now be read with the festival already in mind.

Neither letter, however, relates to the events narrated in the history. The first simply calls on the Egyptian Jews to celebrate the feast, apparently in thanksgiving for the restoration of the sacrifices, but there is no mention of the desecration by Antiochus, nor of Judas's rescue of the temple and its purification. The second letter, too, is addressed to the Jews of Egypt, and is a retelling of beliefs about the sacred fire for the temple sacrifices, miraculously renewed when the temple was restored after the exile. The letter illustrates that God continues to care for the temple, even when all seems lost. Both letters were later additions to the abridged history, probably because of the mention of the feast. The parallel with the renewal of the sacred lamps at Judas's restoration may also have influenced the addition of the second letter to the history.

Other letters, however, are included within both 1 and 2 Maccabees, as is typical of history writing. Ancient historians were aware of the need to provide proper documentation to support their position.⁹ Both books of the Maccabees contain several letters and other documentation, although there are some modern questions of authenticity around them. Besides the two added to the preface, the letters in 2 Maccabees give a good idea of how such documentation is used.

The author of 2 Maccabees has included a set of four letters (11:16–38), which together support the claim that the king granted all the requests made by Judas through Lysias (v. 15). The first, a letter to the Jews from Lysias, the king's regent, affirms that the king

---

8. Although v. 9 speaks of the festival of booths (Sukkot), a fall festival in September-October, the dating of this festival in Chislev (December) points to the feast of Dedication, as the context also implies.
9. Cf. the letter from the Jerusalem leadership to the churches in Antioch, Syria, and Cilicia (Acts 15:23–29).

has been informed of certain matters, and that Lysias will continue to support the Jews if they remain loyal (vv. 16–21). The next two are from King Antiochus to Lysias (vv. 22–26) and to the Jews (vv. 27–33), confirming that the Jewish customs be permitted. Lastly, a letter from the Romans to the Jews seems to support the decisions noted in the previous two (vv. 34–38). Although there is some scholarly discussion about how the letters relate to the actual chronology of events, the author understood them as referring to the situation at hand, and so included them as supporting documentation. Here we shall look more closely at the third letter.

2 Macc 11:27–33

27. …King Antiochus to the senate of the Jews and to the other Jews, greetings. 28. If you are well, it is as we desire. We also are in good health. 29. Menelaus has informed us that you wish to return home and look after your own affairs. 30. Therefore those who go home by the thirtieth of Xanthicus will have our pledge of friendship and full permission 31. for the Jews to enjoy their own food and laws, just as formerly, and none of them shall be molested in any way for what may have been done in ignorance. 32. And I have also sent Menelaus to encourage you. 33. Farewell. The one hundred forty-eighth year, Xanthicus fifteenth.[10]

This letter, as the others, follows the usual epistolary style. The structure is the same as that of Paul's letters in the New Testament, although Paul's letters are much longer. The sender's name comes first, followed by that of the recipient (compare, for example, Paul's letter to Philemon, vv. 1–2). The greeting is standard (in Greek, *chairein*), as is the polite expression of good wishes; in Christian letters, this came to be replaced by "grace *(charis)* and peace be with you" and by a thanksgiving to God (Phlm 3–7). The body of the letter determines its length—here, we are dealing with business correspondence while Paul's letters deal with a range of matters

10. March, 164 B.C.E.

92

concerning the Christian community. The typical closing is a simple "farewell," replaced in Christian letters with an expression such as "grace be with you" (Phlm 25).

In the context, the king's letter forms part of a chain of correspondence, allowing the Jews to practice their own customs without harassment. Because of the previous letter (vv. 22–26), the author thought the king in this letter also was Antiochus V, for whom Lysias was regent at first (10:11; 11:1). According to the date of the letter, however, Antiochus IV was still living. The historian has confused the order of events. We may quibble about the historian's accuracy, but the principle remains: He included such documents as seemed appropriate to the account, in this case to support the idea that Lysias and Antiochus V were well disposed towards the Jews. But we see illustrated here the difficulty for modern readers in adjudging the date and authenticity of ancient letters.

Another letter in 2 Maccabees has quite a different function, set in the context of the death of Antiochus. According to this legendary story, Antiochus was stricken with a painful illness of the bowels, accompanied by decay, worms, and stench—a suitable ending for one who had desecrated God's temple (9:5–12). Antiochus recognized that his arrogance had brought him to this pass and made haste to free Jerusalem and its inhabitants from his demands (vv. 13–17). At this point, the king drew up a letter to the Jewish community, urging them to support his son in his turn (vv. 18–27). The letter does not fit the context well: The king refers to his illness but hardly in terms of the agonies described and recalls "with affection" the "esteem and good will" of the Jewish community. Although the details of the king's last illness may have been imaginatively construed for dramatic purposes, the letter may well have been sent to loyalist Jewish supporters, who could be expected to support the heir after the death of Antiochus. Here, however, it acts as an appropriate deathbed farewell to the Jewish community from a subdued king, not unlike the role of speeches in ancient history writing.

Whereas 2 Maccabees contains only these few letters, the author of 1 Maccabees seems to have had access to a considerable archive. The historian quotes and refers to letters, decrees, and treaties, copies of which are kept on file:

> Now therefore take care to make a copy of this, and let it be given to Jonathan and put up in a conspicuous place on the holy mountain. (11:37)

> And they gave orders to inscribe this decree on bronze tablets, to put them up in a conspicuous place in the precincts of the sanctuary, and to deposit copies of them in the treasury, so that Simon and his sons might have them. (14:48–49)

> They also sent a copy of these things to the high priest Simon. (15:24)

Several of the letters indicate the support that the Seleucid king Demetrius gave to Jonathan (10:18–20, 25–45; 11:30–37) and Simon (13:36–40; 15:1–9); others are produced to show that the Hasmoneans could operate more internationally. The author includes copies of Jonathan's correspondence to and from the Greek state of Sparta (12:5–18 and 19–23), as for instance the renewal of the Spartan alliance with Simon after Jonathan's death:

> This is a copy of the letter that the Spartans sent: The ruler and the city of the Spartans to the high priest Simon and to the elders and the priests and the rest of the Jewish people, our brothers, greetings. The envoys who were sent to our people have told us about your glory and honor, and we rejoiced at their coming. We have recorded what they said in our public decrees, as follows, "Numenius son of Antiochus and Antipater son of Jason, envoys of the Judeans, have come to us to renew their friendship with us. It has pleased our people to receive these men with honor and to put a copy of their words in the public archives, so that the people of Sparta may have

a record of them. And they have sent a copy of this to the high priest Simon." (14:20–23)

The Romans, too, were supporters of the Judeans. The author summarizes their history and characteristics, although he is not quite accurate in the details (8:1–16), before giving an account of the embassy to Rome, "a very long journey" (8:19). A copy of the Romans' treaty is attached (8:21–32).

Copies of letters and decrees are included in the histories as evidence of the events described and to support the author's interpretation of those events. The writer of 2 Maccabees wants to show how well disposed Antiochus V was to Jews in contrast to his father; the author of 1 Maccabees wants to show how well connected the Hasmonean family is, taking their place on the international stage as worthy rulers of an independent nation. But documents can also be used like speeches, to give a character the opportunity to express sentiments or motivations appropriate to the situation. Occasionally, the author may feel free to compose a suitable document in the interests of the history as a whole. The purpose is not to deceive but to develop or expand an interpretation of people or events.

Because the historian of 1 Maccabees has included such a wealth of documentation, including official correspondence, much of it affirming the authority of the Hasmoneans, it has been suggested that he was probably commissioned by a later Hasmonean ruler, possibly Alexander Jannaeus, to produce an authorized version of the Hasmonean rise to power. If there were any opposition, this history would set the record straight about the Hasmoneans' right and suitability to rule. The author of 2 Maccabees, on the other hand, apparently did not have the same access to official archives, and perhaps it was of less importance. The "unofficial" history is more of a people's history, recounting the resistance of individuals, concentrating on spiritual achievements rather than political. It also includes much legendary material, perhaps in part to compensate for lack of archival resources but perhaps also because these stories aptly express the theology of the Hasidean movement to which the author most likely belonged.

Since the way in which a history is narrated is as significant as what is narrated, we shall continue to explore in the following chapter how language and style also contribute to historiography.

For Further Reading

Michael Duggan, *The Consuming Fire* (San Francisco: Ignatius Press, 1991), pp. 503–511.

George W. E. Nickelsburg, "1 and 2 Maccabees: Same Story, Different Meaning," *Concordia Theological Monthly* 42 (1971), 515–526.

For Further Study

1. In 1 Maccabees, compare the death of Alexander with the death of Antiochus, looking for patterns in structure and language; alternatively, compare the accounts of the death of Antiochus in 1 and 2 Maccabees.

2. Explore the relationship of the Hasmoneans to the Romans, through the eyes of 1 Maccabees.

3. To what extent does the use of letters compare with the use of speeches in biblical history writing?

8

POLITICS AND PIETY

The books of Maccabees have different interpretations of the causes behind the events that befell Jerusalem and its temple in the reign of Antiochus IV. First Maccabees assesses the rebellion in the context of the rise of the Hasmonean dynasty. It attributes the cause of the attack on the temple and subsequent rebellion to the conquests and hellenizing policies of Alexander the Great, brought to their logical conclusion with the desecration of the temple. The Hasmoneans were the ones who liberated the temple and the city from foreign domination and founded a new dynasty of kings and high priests. Second Maccabees, on the other hand, concentrates on the actions of Judas Maccabeus and his liberation and restoration of the temple, attributing the cause of Judea's problems ultimately to the corruption of the high priesthood. The author of 1 Maccabees takes a more political view of the situation, while the author of 2 Maccabees holds a more religious perspective. The differing perspectives are found not only in what they say, but also in how they say it.

The Style of 1 Maccabees:
In the Footsteps of the Bible

One of the most interesting—and revealing—aspects of 1 Maccabees is the way the author links the account of the Hasmoneans with the histories of the kings of Judah and other heroes. By using the earlier histories as models, the author is asking the reader to look at the present account in continuity with the great events of days gone by. The Hasmoneans are to be seen not as petty rulers of a small nation, but as major actors in an ongoing history. We see this when the language of 1 Maccabees imitates the style of the books of Kings, as, for example, in the concluding verses of the book:

> The rest of the acts of John and his wars and the brave deeds that he did, and the building of the walls that he completed, and his achievements, are written in the annals of his high priesthood, from the time that he became high priest after his father. (1 Macc 16:23–24)

The phrasing is similar to that found frequently in the books of Kings as the concluding formula of a king's reign, as the following examples show:

> Now the rest of the acts of Jeroboam, how he warred and how he reigned, are written in the Book of the Annals of the Kings of Israel. (1 Kgs 14:19)

> Now the rest of the acts of Rehoboam, and all that he did, are they not written in the Book of the Annals of the Kings of Judah? (1 Kgs 14:29)

> Now the rest of the acts that Jehoash did, his might, and how he fought with King Amaziah of Judah, are they not written in the Book of the Annals of the Kings of Israel? (2 Kgs 14:15)

> The rest of the deeds of Hezekiah, all his power, how he made the pool and the conduit and brought water into the city, are they not written in the Book of the Annals of the Kings of Judah? (2 Kgs 20:20)

This formulaic conclusion is found not only at the end of John's rule, but also earlier in the book, at the end of Judas's career:

> Now the rest of the acts of Judas, and his wars and the brave deeds that he did, and his greatness, have not been recorded, but they were very many. (1 Macc 9:22)

The author may have faced the difficulty of lack of documentation for Judas, but the formula is utilized nonetheless. The word pattern is immediately recognizable to anyone who knows the books of Kings.

There is something else to notice about the death of Judas. Having fallen in battle, Judas is buried by his brothers Jonathan and Simon, and all Israel mourned: "How is the mighty fallen, the savior of Israel!" (1 Macc 9:21). Here the historian quotes the lament of David for Saul and Jonathan. They, too, died in battle and all Israel mourned them. The lament that David ordered to be sung had as its refrain "How the mighty have fallen!" (2 Sam 1:17–27). Perhaps the connection of names with the first Jonathan, Saul's son and David's sworn friend, led the author to recall David's lament. Just as David took over kingship from Saul, so does Jonathan take over leadership from Judas. In the story of David, all Israel gathered to make him their king (2 Sam 5:3); here in Maccabees, the friends of Judas urge Jonathan to take up leadership (9:28–31). So again the Maccabees are subtly likened to the nation's first kings. They, too, had to struggle against enemies to establish an independent kingdom.

There are also some reminiscences of the Book of Judges, another book that narrates stories of great Israelite leaders, who saved the people from their oppressors. In the Book of Judges, the announcement of the defeat of the enemy is often followed by the phrase "the land had rest" (Judg 3:11, 30; 5:31; 8:28). 1 Maccabees also uses this phrase at key points, after the defeat of Nicanor (7:50) and after the death of Alcimus, the high priest appointed by the king, when the Seleucid army withdrew to Syria (9:57). It is also said of Jonathan that he "began to judge the people," the same expression used of the warrior saviors of Israel in Judges. These echoes are few, but catch the eye and ear of anyone who knows the Book of Judges.

By placing the Hasmonean family in the company of the great warriors and heroes of Israel, the historian is interpreting their actions in the light of Israel's sacred history. As in the past God acted through the deeds of these great men, so too does God act through Mattathias and his sons. Success is achieved by action in the light of the sacred law.

The most telling parallel between the Maccabees and the heroes of the past, however, is the modeling of Mattathias on the priest Phinehas. The story of Phinehas is found in the Book of Numbers, in the context of the Israelites' journeying through the wilderness. God's punishment is threatened because the Israelites are turning to alien gods (Num 25:1–3). As you read the two passages, notice the similarities between them. What is the effect?

Num 25:6–9

6. Just then one of the Israelites came and brought a Midianite woman into his family, in the sight of Moses and in the sight of the whole congregation of the Israelites, while they were weeping at the entrance of the tent of meeting. 7. When Phinehas son of Eleazar, son of Aaron the priest, saw it, he got up and left the congregation. Taking a spear in his hand, 8. he went after the Israelite man into the tent, and pierced the two of them, the Israelite and the woman, through the belly. So the plague was stopped among the people of Israel. 9. Nevertheless those that died by the plague were twenty-four thousand. 10. The LORD spoke to Moses, saying: 11. "Phinehas son of Eleazar, son of Aaron the priest, has turned back my wrath from the Israelites by manifesting such zeal among them on my behalf that in my jealousy I did not consume the Israelites. 12. Therefore say, 'I hereby grant him my covenant of peace. 13. It shall be for him and for his descendants after him a covenant of perpetual priesthood, because he was zealous for his God, and made atonement for the Israelites.'"

1 Macc 2:23–26

23. When he had finished speaking these words, a Jew came forward in the sight of all to offer sacrifice on the altar in Modein, according to the king's command. 24.

When Mattathias saw it, he burned with zeal and his heart was stirred. He gave vent to righteous anger; he ran and killed him on the altar. 25. At the same time he killed the king's officer who was forcing them to sacrifice, and he tore down the altar. 26. Thus he burned with zeal for the law, just as Phinehas did against Zimri son of Salu.

Whatever we may think about the way Phinehas and Mattathias expressed their zeal, the parallel is made explicit. Imitating the earlier action, Mattathias and his sons raise the cry to summon "everyone who is zealous for the law." The rebellion has begun.

But there is more: Phinehas is a model not just because of his zeal, but also because of his reward, "a covenant of perpetual priesthood." Mattathias and his sons are from a priestly family, and indeed by the end of the history both Simon, the last surviving son of Mattathias, and Simon's own son, Jonathan, will have held the high priestly office. On his deathbed, Mattathias already looks forward to this outcome. In his final speech, the patriarch of the family lists Israelite heroes who were noted for their faithfulness, including Phinehas "our ancestor," who "because he was deeply zealous received the covenant of everlasting priesthood" (2:54), exactly as the Lord had promised in Num 25:13. Through Mattathias, the history is at pains to demonstrate that the Hasmoneans have a legitimate claim to the high priesthood, confirmed by their zeal for the law. It is in fact on this note that the historian chooses to close the work, with a reference to the high priesthood of Jonathan and Simon (16:24).

The deathbed speech of Mattathias also hearkens back to the deathbed speech of the patriarch Jacob (Gen 49). He, too, addressed his sons, assessing them and looking forward to their achievements. No less does Mattathias address his sons but in his case holding out the patriarchs and other heroes as models. In so many ways, then, the author of 1 Maccabees weaves links with the biblical leaders, patriarchs, and kings, to point to the significance of the Hasmonean house: a dynasty like that of David, and a promised high priesthood. According to 1 Maccabees, this family has the best credentials for taking over the leadership of the Jews. The Hasmonean dynasty is in place.

History Makes a Theological Point (1): God Is with the Hasmoneans

The author of 1 Maccabees takes a political stance regarding the role of the Hasmoneans, but there is a theology at work here, too. Both 1 and 2 Maccabees share the view that God supports the Jewish cause. But while 2 Maccabees understands God to take direct action in human affairs, 1 Maccabees understands divine intervention happening through chosen individuals, such as Abraham and Jacob, Joshua and David. That is one reason why these ancestors are invoked either directly, as in Mattathias's final speech, or indirectly by allusion or parallel.

The most important positions of 1 Maccabees are laid out in the first two chapters of the book. It is not only the political situation of Alexander's hellenized empire that was a cause of trouble for Judea, but the wickedness of Antiochus, the "sinful root" of the Seleucids (1:10) and of "certain renegades" (1:11–14). Apostate Jews also contribute to the problem. They ally themselves with Gentiles "to do evil" (1:14), that is, they become hellenized, eschewing circumcision—the sign of the covenant (Gen 17:10–11)—and generally observing Gentile ways. And they ally themselves with Seleucid power when a garrison is placed in the city (1:34). Abandonment of the covenant is a major cause of the troubles which descend upon Jerusalem and "Israel," the faithful Jews. The author even includes laments, like those in the Psalms and prophetic books, as reflections on the sad state of Jerusalem and her people (1:24–28, 36–40). But deliverance comes through human action, and military action at that.

What options did the people have? Jews were usually reluctant to oppose authority in the belief that God put rulers in place or removed them. In spite of hellenization, Jews got along well with their overlords, as long as they were allowed to maintain their traditional way of life. Antiochus changed all that. He not only despoiled the temple, but went so far as to set up a pagan cult there, and he proscribed Jewish practices. The choice was to adapt or to suffer the consequences. Some adapted: "Many of the people, everyone who forsook the law, joined them, and they did evil in the land" (1:52). But many others refused, holding onto their sacred traditions, moving into the wilderness regions if they were able. The author describes what they died for, which in turn tells us what was important to those who saw themselves as faithful: possessing the book of the covenant, or the book of the law (1:57), having their children circumcised (1:60–61), and not eating unclean food (1:62): "They chose to die rather than to be defiled by food or to profane the holy covenant; and they did die" (1:63).

Mattathias breaks out of this pattern when he kills the unnamed Jew and the king's officer. We have already seen that he is filled with "zeal" and "righteous anger," and in this he is compared to Phinehas, who was rewarded with an eternal covenant of priesthood. The actions of Mattathias are interpreted as condoned by God. To put it another way, Mattathias apparently fulfills divine will by his zealous rage.

Since speeches in a history are usually provided to supply what the historian thought appropriate to the character in the circumstances, they thus actually reveal the author's interpretation of events. The speech of Mattathias proclaims the rationale for his actions:

> But Mattathias answered and said in a loud voice: "Even if all the nations that lie under the rule of the king obey him, and have chosen to obey his commandments, everyone of them abandoning the religion of their ancestors, I and my sons and my brothers will continue to live by the covenant of our ancestors. Far be it from us to desert the law and the ordinances. We will not obey the king's words by turning aside from our religion to the right hand or to the left." (2:19–22)

Then Mattathias kills the renegade Jew and the royal official, calling on all like-minded people to join him: "Let everyone who is zealous for the law and supports the covenant come out with me!" (2:27).

Thus the Maccabean uprising begins. In response to the implied question, "Is it permitted to take up arms against authority?" the answer is "yes," on the principle that adherence to God's commands supersedes obedience to the king. Not only does this condone the revolt, it also condones attacking fellow Jews who do not conform to the rebels' position:

> They organized an army, and struck down sinners and renegades in their wrath; the survivors fled to the Gentiles for safety. And Mattathias and his friends went around and tore down the altars; they forcibly circumcised all the uncircumcised boys that they found within the borders of Israel. They hunted down the arrogant and the work prospered in their hands. They rescued the law out of the hands of the Gentiles and kings, and they never let the sinner gain the upper hand. (2:44–48)

By offering Mattathias as a praiseworthy example, the history affirms that the Hasmonean challenge to Seleucid rule was lawful and even required of those who would remain faithful to the covenant.

There is a further problem to be resolved, however. Is it permitted to fight on the Sabbath? The author includes a story that illustrates this dilemma. Some of the faithful living in the wilderness to escape the royal officials were hunted and discovered. The king's troops lined up for battle, but on the Sabbath day, giving the Jews an ultimatum. They, however, refused to fight on the Sabbath and so all died in the ensuing attack (2:29–38). These Jews represent the "no" side of the question. The response of Mattathias and his supporters, however, is more pragmatic and positive. Yes, it is lawful to defend ourselves against aggressors, even on the Sabbath, lest the whole people be destroyed.[1] That the Maccabees are ultimately successful both in liberating Jerusalem and

---

1. This principle was invoked in the Yom Kippur War (1973), when the modern State of Israel was attacked on the holiest day of the year, in the belief that Israel could not respond. On the contrary, Israel not only mobilized quickly but won the war.

Judea and in rededicating the temple only proves that they were right to espouse these principles of resistance and defense.

It was clear to the writer—and no doubt to the Hasmoneans—that God was on their side. Indeed that thought is voiced later in the history. On one occasion, Judas with three thousand men and inadequate weaponry prepares for battle against the Gentile general Gorgias, who has a full contingent of both infantry and cavalry all well trained. Judas's pre-battle speech expresses the Hasmonean perspective:

> But Judas said to those who were with him, "Do not fear their numbers or be afraid when they charge. Remember how our ancestors were saved at the Red Sea, when Pharaoh with his forces pursued them. And now, let us cry to Heaven,[2] to see whether he will favor us and remember his covenant with our ancestors and crush this army before us today. Then all the Gentiles will know that there is one who redeems and saves Israel." (4:8–11)

Against the odds, the Jews win the battle, and seize rich plunder from the enemy camp: gold, silver, and richly dyed cloth.[3] They return singing hymns and praises to Heaven: "Thus Israel had a great deliverance that day" (4:25).

Some other Jews, thinking to follow the example of Judas and his brothers, faced the Seleucid forces outside Jamnia, but were routed, suffering great loss of life. The reason for their defeat was obvious to the writer: "But they did not belong to the family through whom deliverance was given to Israel" (5:62). The last phrase is significant; deliverance is given through the Maccabee brothers. That

---

2. 1 Maccabees rarely speaks directly of God, but prefers to use the term *Heaven*. This reverential mode of speaking can be seen also in Matthew's Gospel, especially in the term "kingdom of heaven," whereas Luke's Gospel uses "kingdom of God."
3. Details like these tell us the nature of the story: A military camp may have traveled with supplies, but hardly on this scale.

is, divine purpose is achieved through human activity, but only through those who are chosen.

Thus the Hasmoneans are vindicated. They are successful in their revolt against the Seleucid Empire, they are right to defend themselves against a wicked king and on the Sabbath, and only those who are allied with them will enjoy the same success. Yet it is made clear that all this is accomplished by God's will and assistance. And finally, when they do achieve the high priesthood, this will be because of Mattathias's zeal for the law.

History Makes a Theological Point (2): God Works Wonders

While 1 Maccabees understands God to work through human activity, 2 Maccabees claims that God intervenes directly in human affairs. Military exploits are placed in the context of prayer and piety. The author does this by including stories of visions and miracles, which give an entirely different tone to the book. In fact, the epitomist chooses to begin the digest version of the history with a story of a miraculous event.

The whole of 2 Maccabees 3 concerns the attempt by a royal official, Heliodorus, to attack the temple's integrity by expropriating temple funds. What happens, and how the story is told, will set in high relief the centrality and sanctity of the temple for the Jews (as well as for the author). A certain Simon claimed that the treasury contained vast wealth not related to the sacrifice expenses, which the king could get his hands on. To the king's envoy Heliodorus, the high priest Onias insisted that the deposits were greatly overstated, and moreover belonged to widows and orphans as well as to a particular businessman.[4]

And he [Onias] said that it was utterly impossible that wrong should be done to those who had trusted in the

---

4. Temples in the ancient world also operated as banks, a safe place to keep money and valuables, protected (most of the time) by fear of the gods, or in this case, God.

holiness of the place and in the sanctity and inviolability of the temple that is honored throughout the whole world. (3:12)

Heliodorus nevertheless was about to confiscate the money. In the meantime, priests and people responded by prayer and supplication to the Lord to preserve the temple's integrity.

But as Heliodorus approaches the treasury, he experiences a heavenly vision of an armed rider on a horse and two young men who flog Heliodorus until he falls senseless to the ground and has to be carried off, "this man who had just entered the aforesaid treasury with a great retinue and all his bodyguard but was now unable to help himself" (v. 28). All are amazed at the power of God (vv. 24, 28). Lest anyone miss the point, the narrative continues:

While he lay prostrate, speechless because of divine intervention and deprived of any hope of recovery, they praised the Lord who had acted marvelously for his own place. And the temple, which a little while before was full of fear and disturbance, was filled with joy and gladness, now that the Almighty Lord had appeared. (vv. 29–30)

Of course, Onias intercedes for Heliodorus, so as not to upset the king, and Heliodorus is left not only healed but fully conscious that he has experienced the power of God. The moral of the story is two-fold, that no one can breach the temple's sanctity with impunity and that God intervenes in miraculous ways.

Other visions occur throughout the book, usually in association with a battle scene. An apparition of cavalry in battle array is seen over the city for forty days, clearly some sort of omen (5:2–4). In the midst of battle, another vision reveals five horsemen leading the Jews and guarding Judas from harm. These riders attack the enemy, throwing them into confusion and blinding them; the enemy suffers overwhelming casualties (10:29–31). Yet another vision is seen by Judas and his men, of a horseman clothed in white, leading them into battle (11:6–10). In 2 Macc 15:12–16, Judas relates to his followers a vision, or dream, in which the saintly priest Onias appears to him together with the prophet Jeremiah. Jeremiah gives Judas a golden sword with which to strike the enemy.

If the epitomist is trying to produce an abbreviated version, why include the story of Heliodorus? What does it have to do with the history of Judas Maccabeus? The answer is, everything. The focus of 2 Maccabees is the temple, its profanation, and its purification. Judas is the hero of the story, of course, but it is his religious significance that has priority. The cautionary story of Heliodorus prepares the reader/listener for what is to come: The desecration of the temple is indeed shocking but God will intervene to restore the holy place and to punish the perpetrator of such a deed. As we have already learned, Antiochus will eventually fall ill of the most offensive illness, rotting away from the inside, crawling with worms and stinking of decay, a fitting end for the man who dared to bring pagan worship into the sanctuary, and he is shown as recognizing what he has done (9:5–12).

Why, though, did God not intervene to save the temple before it was desecrated, as happened in the case of Heliodorus, and before so many people suffered and died for their faithfulness? The author responds with a further point:

> But if it had not happened that they [the inhabitants of Jerusalem] were involved in many sins, this man would have been flogged and turned back from his rash act as soon as he came forward, just as Heliodorus had been, whom King Seleucus sent to inspect the treasury. (5:18)

According to 2 Maccabees, it was the sinfulness of many Jews that roused the anger of God, and allowed Antiochus to proceed with his attacks on the people. This conforms to the theology of the book that lays the blame primarily on neglect of the law and abandonment of the covenant. Antiochus could not have acted as he did without this precondition.

To appreciate the impact of the story of Heliodorus in the context of the whole book, we return to the prologue, where the epitomist sets out his plan.

2 Macc 2:19–32

19. The story of Judas Maccabeus and his brothers, and the purification of the great temple, and the dedication of the altar, 20. and further the wars against Antiochus Epiphanes and his son Eupator, 21. *and the appearances that came from heaven to those who fought bravely for Judaism,* so that though few in number they seized the whole land and pursued the barbarian hordes, 22. and regained the possession of the temple famous throughout the world, and liberated the city, and re-established the laws that were about to be abolished, while the Lord with great kindness became gracious to them—23. all this, which has been set forth by Jason of Cyrene in five volumes, we shall attempt to condense into a single book.

If we look at the interests of the epitomist, we see that the story of Judas is set in the context of the temple and that the wars against Antiochus are accompanied by "appearances from heaven." The outcome is the repossession of the temple and the re-establishment of the laws, the political achievements are of little or no interest. Military power takes a backseat to piety and cannot succeed without it or clear assistance from Heaven.

Understandably, the piety of Judas is given more attention than in 1 Maccabees, where indeed he does pray and he obviously is an observer of the law. But in 2 Maccabees he is presented as careful about clean and unclean foods, in the wilderness living on what could be found growing in the wilderness (5:27); he prepares for war with prayer and fasting (13:10–12) and with dust and sackcloth (10:25); leaves decisions in the hands of God (13:14); leads his troops to battle with prayer (15:21–27); and keeps the Sabbath (8:26–27;12:38). Throughout, there is constant reference to trust in God and to the need to fight for the law and the temple. This version of Judas is precisely the right kind of hero for the author of 2 Maccabees.

The Style of 2 Maccabees:
Direct Appeal to the Reader

Prominent in the style of 2 Maccabees is the appeal to emotion, quite unlike the style of the first history, which has a matter-of-fact tone. Starting again with the story of Heliodorus in 2 Macc 3, notice how the text creates the atmosphere with attention to detail:

> People also hurried out of their houses in crowds.
> …Women, girded with sackcloth under their breasts,
> thronged the streets. Some of the young women who
> were kept indoors ran together to the gates, and some to
> the walls, while others peered out of the windows.
> (3:18–19)

Not content with a statement about the anxiety in the city, the author fills out the picture of a populace in "no little distress" (v. 13), gathering anxiously in crowds, abandoning the normal restrictions. The vocabulary is full of feeling:

> To see the appearance of the high priest was to be
> wounded at heart, for his face and the change in his color
> disclosed the anguish of his soul. For terror and bodily
> trembling had come over the man, which plainly showed
> to those who looked at him the pain lodged in his heart.
> (3:16–17)

The people are "pitiable," the high priest full of "great anguish" (v. 21). What could possibly relieve such distress? Priests and people are helpless before the authority of the king.

The history relates the harrowing suffering of those who remain faithful to the Torah, including the story of Eleazar who was tortured, perhaps beaten to death, and that of the legendary seven sons who were martyred one by one before their mother's eyes. The speeches of the mother and her seven sons express the theology of the Hasideans, including observance of the law, punishment of the wicked, and belief in resurrection (7:9, 11, 14, 23). All this heightens the suffering of the people, to show how much the faithful are prepared to bear rather than abandon the law. They even prefer to die rather than profane the Sabbath—here we have the same incident as in 1 Maccabees, but given as an example of fidelity for "that most holy day" (6:11). In 1 Maccabees, Mattathias rejected this type of piety in favor of self-defense (1 Macc 2:39).

Appeal to emotion is a direct address to the reader, to draw us closer into the story of those who are suffering. It is related to another aspect of style, the voice of the writer. In the previous chapter we noted how the author of 2 Maccabees, the epitomist, set out in a prologue what we should expect to find in the book. Looking at the prologue again, we realize that the author speaks personally to the reader, using the editorial "we": "we shall attempt to condense" the work of Jason, "we have aimed to please," "let us begin," and so forth. The writer, moreover, makes personal comments about himself: It has been hard work, which "calls for sweat and loss of sleep," but this is gladly undertaken to produce something beneficial (2:25–28). The same direct address is found at the close of the book, where the author expresses hope that the work was well done (15:38–39). Much more than in 1 Maccabees, the writer is present to us in a personal way.

Throughout 2 Maccabees, the writer breaks into the flow of the narrative with analysis, comments, and exhortation. Such is the case in 4:17, where the author makes a little admonition: "It is no light thing to show irreverence to the divine laws—a fact that later events will make clear." This is in reference to the increased hellenization under Antiochus, the "wickedness" of Jason the high priest, and the neglect of the temple. In keeping with the theology of the book, we are forewarned that dread events will come upon the people of Jerusalem because of all this (v. 16).

Yet another passage self-consciously interrupts the narrative line to address the reader directly.

111

2 Macc 6:12–17

12. Now I urge those who read this book not to be depressed by such calamities, but to recognize that these punishments were designed not to destroy but to discipline our people. 13. In fact, it is a sign of great kindness not to let the impious alone for long, but to punish them immediately. 14. For in the case of the other nations the Lord waits patiently to punish them until they have reached the full measure of their sins; but he does not deal this way with us, 15. in order that he may not take vengeance on us afterward when our sins have reached their height. 16. Therefore he never withdraws his mercy from us. Although he disciplines us with calamities, he does not forsake his own people. 17. Let what we have said serve as a reminder; we must go on with the story.

This little insert speaks for itself. It is a word of encouragement as well as explanation for why the Jews had to suffer the dreadful persecutions of Antiochus. In keeping with the theology of 2 Maccabees, it is not simply that Antiochus is an oppressor, but that the people have sinned. God moves swiftly to punish the people in order to prevent even worse happening.

Overall, we are quite conscious of the writer's presence. The book does not simply relate the story of Judas Maccabeus but speaks to us, the readers, directly and personally. We are called into the narrative to experience the same feelings as the actors. We are not only expected to learn something of what happened but are also invited, perhaps expected, to share the writer's perspective and faith.

But Is It history?

Any history has its ideology, that is, its own framework of ideas and beliefs within which it operates and which it promotes by its interpretation of events. Thus, 1 Maccabees views the Maccabean revolt as the start of the Hasmonean rise to power, aided by God because the Hasmoneans pursued the right interpretation of Torah observance. And 2 Maccabees sees the attack on Jerusalem and the temple as punishment for abandonment of the Torah. The subsequent restoration of the temple is accomplished by unambiguous heavenly assistance, evidence that God comes to the rescue of the people and the holy place. Sometimes the ideology of a text is clearly expressed, as in the preface to 2 Maccabees, and sometimes it is simply assumed and worked out in the course of the narrative, as is the case with 1 Maccabees. And in the ancient world, facts and chronology sometimes take second place in the interests of a compelling argument or a satisfactory structuring of material. Identifying the ideology of the author, whether explicit or implicit, is an important key to understanding the whole work.

Style, ideology, purpose, and scope—all are interconnected. We have made a brief foray into these aspects to give an idea of the competence of the writers and their creativity in interpreting and writing about historical events. Are 1 and 2 Maccabees in fact histories? In spite of their—to us moderns—unfamiliar approach, not to mention their inaccuracies, the answer is yes. Both authors have the intent to tell us about the past, to order events chronologically, to search for causes and to assess the impact of what happened. That they have a theological interpretation is no surprise: Both writers come from a milieu that is convinced God is at work in the world. As an official history of the dynasty, 1 Maccabees comes closer to the kind of history we moderns are comfortable with and demonstrates that ancient historians were as interested in recording and narrating events as we are. In style, it is modeled on the Old Testament histories. The shorter popular history, 2 Maccabees, is as interested in promoting the sanctity of the temple and offering examples of piety for the reader as it is in relating what happened. In style it follows Hellenistic histories. Are they reliable witnesses to what actually happened? There we would have to exercise caution. Certainly for the general outline of events both histories give a reasonable account; the problems are in the details. At that point we would have to turn to the scholarly research for clarification.

For Further Reading

Harold W. Attridge, "Historiography" in *Jewish Writings of the Second Temple Period,* Michael E. Stone, ed. (Philadelphia: Fortress Press, 1984), pp.157–184. Scholarly but accessible.

Michael Duggan, *The Consuming Fire* (San Francisco: Ignatius Press, 1991), pp. 511–520.

Neil J. McEleney, "1–2 Maccabees" in *The New Jerome Biblical Commentary,* pp. 421–425.

For Further Study

1. Examine the story of the mother and her seven sons (2 Macc 7:1–41) for its structure and language or the role of the speeches. What kind of story is this?

2. How and to what purpose does the author of 1 Maccabees use poetry in the context of the history?

9

FROM ENTRANCE TO EXILE:
THE DEUTERONOMISTIC HISTORY

So far we have looked at individual books which dealt with limited aspects of history: The Book of Acts reconstructed a history of the first generation of the Christian Church, and the books of Maccabees narrated the rise of the Hasmoneans, each in its own way. We have a different situation in the Old Testament where several books seem to narrate a history of Israel across not just generations, but centuries. The books of Samuel and Kings present a history spanning the entire monarchy of the people of Israel. Scholars, however, have recognized a much longer historical effort starting with the narratives of the books of Joshua and Judges. That is, we have a set of books that narrate a connected history of Israel from the entrance into the land to the final defeat of Jerusalem by the Babylonians, a span of over 700 years according to the inner chronology of the history. This lengthy treatment is shaped by recurrent patterns of language and style and by a theology that is based on the book of Deuteronomy. Thus the whole narrative cycle from Joshua through 2 Kings has been given the title "the Deuteronomistic History."

These books present a continuous narrative from the time Israel enters the promised land to the fall of Jerusalem centuries later.[1] The Book of Joshua relates the conquest of the land of Canaan by Israel under the leadership of Joshua, the successor to Moses, who then apportions territory to the tribes. An unsettled period is narrated in the Book of Judges: Although the land has been given to them, the tribes do not follow the way of Yahweh, Israel's God, and consequently come under the control of various

---

1. The Book of Ruth was inserted at a later date between Judges and 1 Samuel.

enemies. Certain charismatic leaders arise to save the day, but the resulting peace is only temporary and the cycle of oppression continues. In the first book of Samuel, a shift takes place from a leadership of those who judge Israel (the priest Eli and the prophet Samuel) to the establishment of a monarchy. Saul, the first king, turns out to be unsatisfactory and is replaced by David, who will prove to be a model for later generations. The narrative continues into the second book of Samuel, where the story of David is told. Having united the tribes under his rule, David establishes Jerusalem as his capital and makes the preparations for a temple to the God of Israel. His reign is scarred by treachery and rebellion, but he remains faithful to God.

The books of Kings continue the narrative of David's descendants. His immediate successor is his son, Solomon, who has a glorious reputation for wisdom and wealth, and for building the temple, but after his death the nation splits apart. Solomon's son Rehoboam is left with only the small area of Judah while the rest of the nation— the northern tribes—follow Jeroboam as the kingdom of Israel. From this point on, the narrative traces the kings of both Judah and Israel until the conquest of the northern kingdom by the Assyrians. In the same campaign Judah and Jerusalem almost share the same fate but the Assyrian army withdraws, leaving Jerusalem for another day. Later, however, the Assyrians are in their turn conquered by the Babylonian Empire, which eventually does attack Judah; Jerusalem is destroyed. The remaining claimants to the throne of Judah are taken to Babylon, along with some of the population.

The history looks back from the standpoint of the reign of King Josiah, who undertook certain religious reforms in the mid– to late seventh century B.C.E., not long before the fall of Judah to the Babylonian Empire. As a result of Josiah's reforms, the temple was cleared of "foreign" objects that compromised the worship of Yahweh, the God of Israel, and other sanctuaries outside Jerusalem were closed down. The Jerusalem temple became the only legitimate place of sacrifice for the people of the kingdom of Judah.

The biblical book that lays out the vision of Josiah's reforms is Deuteronomy, an early version of which may have been the document so conveniently discovered in Josiah's temple renovations. The movement behind the book and the reforms is known as the Deuteronomistic school or circle. From the perspective of Deuteronomy and the Deuteronomists, worship of Yahweh alone in the Jerusalem temple was something intended from the beginning, commanded by God through Moses when the people first came into possession of the land of Canaan. Modern scholars, however, see it as the climax of a growing monotheistic movement in priestly and prophetic circles, the "Yahweh-alone" party as it is sometimes called. Careful reading of biblical texts and the findings of archaeology point to a more polytheistic society, in which the worship of Israel's God, Yahweh, was significant but not exclusive. The Book of Deuteronomy looks forward to and gives instructions for life in the land, but the central consideration is always right worship of Yahweh, which consists of fidelity to the law and to the uniqueness of the Jerusalem temple.

The history traces the fortunes of the people, Israel, and their leaders against the backdrop of their obedience to the covenant regulations laid out in the book of Deuteronomy. There is therefore a continuity of ideology throughout the work. There is also considerable consistency in language and style. The work is thought to have originated in the same school of thought that produced the Book of Deuteronomy, but the original author is unknown. Most scholars posit a first edition, probably around the time of King Josiah in the seventh century, supplemented and revised by a later hand during the exile of the sixth century. There is scholarly debate around variations of this theory. The term "the Deuteronomist" is used to designate the person who composed or compiled the history.

For our purposes, we shall simply look at the final work—the biblical text as we have it today—and try to discern the patterns which shape the historical work.

History and Chronology

Every history has a chronological framework or, to put it another way, chronological sequence is a way of organizing material especially characteristic of a history. Historians are interested in the order of events because they also inquire into the causes and effects of those events. As we have already seen with the books of Acts and Maccabees, a history is not a mere recital of what happened but is also an interpretation. As a result, we generally think of history as a narrative which makes sense of events in their chronological order.

The Deuteronomistic History presents a sequential account of the people of Israel from the conquest and settlement of the land through the establishment of a monarchy and the subsequent division of the kingdom into Israel in the north and Judah in the south. It narrates the fall of the northern kingdom, then draws to a close with the last kings of Judah and the subjugation of Judah to the Babylonian Empire. The triumphant entry of Israel into the land contrasts with the sad collapse of the nation and the dispersal of the survivors. It is this sequential arrangement which has led readers to understand the books as a history.

Histories also date the events they include. They tell us not only in what order events happened, but also how those events relate to a wider chronological context. Thus in Maccabees, the revolt against Antiochus and the subsequent battles and victories are set in a schema of dating according to the Seleucid emperors. Luke's Gospel sets the chronological context at the beginning, by placing the birth of Jesus in the period of the Roman emperor Augustus, and his ministry in the time of the Roman emperor Tiberius.[2] The Deuteronomistic History has two key dating systems, one that relates to two foundational events—the exodus and the building of

---

2. Luke's dating of the ministry is more specific than the birth, which takes place sometime in the reigns of Augustus (internationally) and Herod (locally). But Luke can date the beginning of John the Baptist's preaching to the "fifteenth year of the reign of Tiberius" (27 C.E.). The ministry of Jesus follows after that.

the temple—and one which correlates the kings of Israel with the kings of Judah.

Our starting point is 1 Kgs 6:1 where, in the context of the building of the temple, a specific time reference is given: "The four hundred eightieth year after the Israelites came out of the land of Egypt, in the fourth year of Solomon's reign over Israel, in the month of Ziv, which is the second month." The writer of this statement obviously considers these two events to be both related and pivotal. The exodus is readily understood as a turning point, but the establishment of the temple as a key event instead of, say, the accession of David is the choice of the historian. It reveals what is significant in the historian's scheme of things. When we look back, we realize that the book of Deuteronomy has consistently looked forward to the founding of the temple and its status as the sole legitimate place of sacrifice. Up to the reigns of David and Solomon, this chronology helps to shape the overall history.

Starting with the Book of Judges will give us some idea of the difficulties inherent in working out the chronology of the Deuteronomistic History. In this book, specific periods of oppression are followed by specific periods of peace, as a hero is "raised up" by God to "save" Israel from the enemy. So for example, we are told that "the Israelites served King Eglon of Moab eighteen years" (Judg 3:14) and that after Ehud saved the people from Moabite oppression, "the land had rest eighty years." The pattern begins with Othniel (3:7–11), and continues with Ehud, Deborah (4:3 and 5:31), Gideon (6:1 and 8:28). After an interruption with the would-be king Abimelech (Chap. 9), another pattern emerges of a list of men who "judged" Israel for specific periods of time (10: 1–5, 12:7–15). The last of the heroes is Samson, said to have "judged" Israel for twenty years.

All told, the periods of oppression add up to 111 years (Judg 3:8, 14; 4:3; 6:1; 10:8; 13:1) while the periods of "rest from the enemies" add up to 200 years (Judg 3:11, 30; 5:31; 8:28). The time periods of individual judges total 96 years, including Samson. A further three years could be included for Abimelech. So far we have accounted for 410 years in the Book of Judges. But in the 480 years

119

since the exodus, according to 1 Kgs 6:1, we also have to include forty years of wilderness wandering, forty years for the priest Eli (1 Sam 4:18), the forty years of David's reign, and four of Solomon to reach the point of the foundation of the temple, at least another 124 years—not counting the time Samuel the prophet judged Israel, which is not specified—for a grand total of 534 years! Either the historian's arithmetic is off, or there has to be another way of thinking about the chronological data.

Chronological Patterns

It may be more helpful to look at the *patterns* in the chronology. We begin with the dating of the temple's foundation. The 480 years from exodus to temple is, of course, forty times twelve, the number of the tribes. This looks more like a symbolic number or time period rather than a factual one and appropriate for a history which regards the building of the temple as the climax of settling the land. The number forty appears frequently in biblical texts as a round number signifying fullness or completion, so forty years indicates something like a generation, or a completed cycle. The people of Israel spent forty years in the wilderness until the exodus generation had died out and a new generation had arisen (Num 32:13).

The forty-year theme is continued in the history prior to the division of the kingdom. So David reigned for forty years as did Solomon (1 Kgs 2:11; 11:42). Prior to the monarchy, Eli the priest is said to have "judged" Israel for forty years, and the hero Samson for twenty years. The pattern is especially noticeable in the Book of Judges, where the periods of rest from the enemies are measured in forty or eighty years for a total of 200 years. The fullness of the periods of "rest" is the result of the faithfulness of the people under the leadership of the savior judges, and David and Solomon, as Israel's greatest kings, could not have reigned for less than a full cycle of years. Clearly these numbers are "round figures," probably symbolic numbers to account for what must have been gaps in the historian's narrative. We should not expect the ancient historian to have had accurate chronological data before an established palace and temple bureaucracy, with both an interest in and a location for systematic record keeping.

Whatever the problems of the chronology, however inaccurate or symbolic its numbers, its presence indicates a historiographic intent on the part of the author. This is what histories do. A modern historian, to be sure, would not substitute symbolic numbers to replace lack of information. The ancient historian, however, is attempting to reconstruct Israel's history with limited resources, although with a rich tradition of stories. Consciously arranging the material in sequence and weaving them into a connected narrative is the stuff of history writing.

While the pattern of forty is perhaps clearer in retrospect, another pattern found in the books of Kings is more easily recognizable (although there are difficulties with the data here too). Each king's accession is given a chronological reference which correlates with his counterpart in the other kingdom, as we see in the examples which follow. Together with other regularly occurring elements, these accession notices create a consistent pattern.[3]

a. Nadab son of Jeroboam began to reign over Israel in the second year of King Asa of Judah; he reigned over Israel two years. (1 Kgs 15:25)

b. In the third year of King Asa of Judah, Baasha son of Ahijah began to reign over all Israel at Tirzah; he reigned twenty-four years. (1 Kgs 15:33)

c. In the thirty-eighth year of King Asa of Judah, Ahab son of Omri began to reign over Israel; Ahab son of Omri reigned over Israel in Samaria twenty-two years. (1 Kgs 16:29)

In the accession notices for the kings of Israel, we are told the king's name and patronymic (his father's name), when he began to reign relative to the current king of Judah, and how long he ruled.

---

3. The same pattern is utilized by the author of 1 Maccabees (9:22; 16:23–24); see Chapter 8 above.

This creates a chain of regnal years which gives scholars a base on which to calculate the absolute chronology in the modern sense. Note, however, that although Nadab is said to have reigned for two years from the second year of Asa of Judah, King Baasha's reign dates from the third year of Asa of Judah. In some dating systems, counting the years of the king's reign begins only with the first New Year; in others, the actual year of accession is year one. In Israel it seems that the king's reign is counted from the actual accession year. So for Nadab, a partial year followed by a partial year is still credited as two years.

The formulas for the kings of Judah are much the same, but include the name of the king's mother and his age at the time of his accession.

a. In the twentieth year of King Jeroboam of Israel, Asa began to reign over Judah; he reigned forty-one years in Jerusalem. His mother's name was Maacah daughter of Abishalom. (1 Kgs 15:9–10)

b. Jehoshaphat son of Asa began to reign over Judah in the fourth year of King Ahab of Israel. Jehoshaphat was thirty-five years old when he began to reign, and he reigned twenty-five years in Jerusalem, His mother's name was Azubah daughter of Shilhi. (1 Kgs 22:41–42)

c. In the twenty-seventh year of King Jeroboam of Israel King Azariah son of Amaziah of Judah began to reign. He was sixteen years old when he began to reign, and he reigned fifty-two years in Jerusalem. His mother's name was Jecoliah of Jerusalem. (2 Kgs 15:1–2)

The accession formulas indicate that the writer has an interest in chronological sequence and that an attempt has been made to associate the sequence of northern kings with that of the southern kings.

From the kind of information in the accession formula, it would appear that the Deuteronomistic historian has acquired data from archival material of some description. Moreover, at the end of each king's reign we find a closing formula, in the same style as the accession formula:

a. Now the rest of the acts of Nadab, and all that he did, are they not written in the Book of the Annals of the Kings of Israel? (1 Kgs 15:31)

b. Now the rest of the acts of Baasha, what he did, and his power, are they not written in the Book of the Annals of the Kings of Israel? Baasha slept with his ancestors, and was buried at Tirzah; and his son Elah succeeded him. (1 Kgs 16:5–6)

c. Now the rest of the acts of Elah, and all that he did, are they not written in the Book of the Annals of the Kings of Israel? (1 Kgs 16:14)

d. Now the rest of the acts of Zimri, and the conspiracy that he made, are they not written in the Book of the Annals of the Kings of Israel? (1 Kgs 16:20)

e. Now the rest of the acts of Omri, and the power that he showed, are they not written in the Book of the Annals of the Kings of Israel? Omri slept with his ancestors, and was buried in Samaria; his son Ahab succeeded him. (1 Kgs 16:27–28)

Several examples have been included here to point out not only the formula itself but also the variations. One thing to notice is that kings of the northern kingdom, Israel, are not always succeeded by their sons—Nadab was killed in conflict with Baasha, who then seized power and had the rest of the family killed; Elah was assassinated by Zimri, who himself only lasted a week. Zimri is still included in the Book of the Annals, however, which suggests that this book may have been a king list of the sort found in the ancient world.

The formula for the kings of Judah is similar:

a. The rest of the acts of Abijam, and all that he did, are they not written in the Book of the Annals of the Kings of Judah? There was war between Abijam and Jeroboam. Abijam slept with his ancestors, and they buried him in the city of David. Then his son Asa succeeded him. (1 Kgs 15:7–8)

b. Now the rest of the acts of Jehoshaphat, and his power that he showed, and how he waged war, are they not written in the Book of the Annals of the Kings of Judah? Jehoshaphat slept with his ancestors and was buried with his ancestors in the city of his father David; his son Jehoram succeeded him. (1 Kgs 22:45, 50)

c. Now the rest of the acts of Azariah, and all that he did, are they not written in the Book of the Annals of the Kings of Judah? Azariah slept with his ancestors; they buried him with his ancestors in the city of David; his son Jotham succeeded him. (2 Kgs 15:6–7).

d. Now the rest of the acts of Jotham, and all that he did, are they not written in the Book of the Annals of the Kings of Judah? Jotham slept with his ancestors, and was buried with his ancestors in the city of David, his ancestor; his son Ahaz succeeded him. (2 Kgs 15:36, 38)

To be noted here is that each king of Judah is succeeded by his son, showing an unbroken line from David and Solomon to the last king of Judah. Each is buried "with his ancestors" in Jerusalem, "the city of David." Besides chronicling the succession of one king to the next, the repetition of the formula also has the effect of emphasizing the stability of the Davidic line, and the connection of the monarchy with Jerusalem, the place where the temple is to be found. The interconnection of monarchy, temple, and continuity of David's dynasty is very important to the Deuteronomistic History.

The uninterrupted succession of the Davidic line must have affirmed for the historian the significant role of David in the history of the people. He is credited with uniting the northern and southern tribes into one kingdom and with making Jerusalem his capital. He is also given some credit for the temple although it was actually built in the reign of his son Solomon. From the perspective of the Deuteronomistic historian, David is the model king, a factor that will recur in the assessment of the monarchy.

Even with the predictable repetition of accession formulas and death notices, modern scholars have found difficulties with the factual chronology of the kings of Judah and Israel. The Deuteronomistic historian seems to have worked with what information was available from existing archival material, the Books of the Annals of the Kings. Unfortunately today we have no way of knowing what precisely these books consisted of. Perhaps they were simply king lists, as have been found in other kingdoms, with some significant events of each reign included. They do not seem to have been full histories and there is no further record of them. The Deuteronomistic History, with all its limitations, is the main historical effort to have come down to us.[4] The task of the modern reader is to recognize the limitations of these books as history while appreciating the enormity of the ancient writer's undertaking.

History writing is also assessment, which is explicit in the Deuteronomistic History. To that aspect we turn in the following chapter.

For Further Reading

Robert B. Coote and Mary P. Coote, *Power, Politics, and the Making of the Bible* (Philadelphia: Fortress Press, 1990), Chapter 9, "Josiah and the Deuteronomists."

Frank Moore Cross, *Canaanite Myth and Hebrew Epic* (Cambridge, MA: Harvard University Press, 1973), Chapter 10, "The Themes of the Book of Kings and the Structure of the Deuteronomistic History."

Michael Duggan, *The Consuming Fire* (San Francisco: Ignatius Press, 1999), Chapter 13.

---

4. The Book of Chronicles covers the same history but is itself based on the Deuteronomistic History.

Morton Smith, *Palestinian Parties and Politics That Shaped the Old Testament* (London: SCM Press, 1987), Chapter 2.

Moshe Weinfeld, "Deuteronomy's Theological Revolution," *Bible Review* XII/1 (February 1996), 38–41, 44–45.

For Further Study

1. Research the difficulties of establishing an accurate chronology of Israelite history.
2. The accession formulas for the kings of Judah include the name of the queen mother. What was the role of the queen mother in the ancient world?

10

"FOR THE SAKE OF DAVID MY SERVANT"

History as Assessment 1: The Kings of Israel

The regnal formulas of the Deuteronomistic History contain more than a straightforward accession or death notice; they also contain the assessment of the king by the historian. Again, it is always instructive to be attentive to the patterns that emerge from the text. We begin with the northern kingdom, Israel:

> Nadab son of Jereboam began to reign over Israel in the second year of King Asa of Judah; he reigned over Israel two years. *He did what was evil in the sight of the LORD, walking in the way of his ancestor and in the sin that he caused Israel to commit.* (1 Kgs 15:25–26)

> In the third year of King Asa of Judah, Baasha son of Ahijah began to reign over all Israel at Tirzah; he reigned twenty-four years. *He did what was evil in the sight of the LORD, walking in the way of Jereboam and in the sin that he caused Israel to commit.* (1 Kgs 15:33–34)

> In the thirty-first year of King Asa of Judah, Omri began to reign over Israel; he reigned for twelve years, six of them in Tirzah. He bought the hill of Samaria from Shemer for two talents of silver; he fortified the hill, and called the city that he built, Samaria, after the name of Shemer, the owner of the hill. *Omri did what was evil in the sight of the LORD; he did more evil than all who were*

before him. For he walked in all the way of Jeroboam son of Nebat, and in the sins that he caused Israel to commit, provoking the LORD, the God of Israel, to anger by their idols. (1 Kgs 16:23–26)

In the thirty-eighth year of King Asa of Judah, Ahab son of Omri began to reign over Israel; Ahab son of Omri reigned over Israel in Samaria twenty-two years. *Ahab son of Omri did evil in the sight of the LORD more than all who were before him.* (1 Kgs 16:29–30)

The italicized phrases show the consistent judgment of the historian for all the kings of the northern kingdom, Israel, that they "did evil in the sight of the LORD" (Yahweh).[1] The expression derives from the ideology of the history, and tells us more about the writer than about the kings. The repeated phrase is a formula applied to every king of Israel, no matter what else is recorded. Further, this "evil" appears to be the "sin" of Jereboam, son of Nebat, the first king of Israel who led the revolt of the ten tribes against Solomon's son, Rehoboam. Jereboam's name turns up frequently in the judgment element of the accession formula. It is his "sin" which the kings of Israel repeat with each new reign. The evil of the northern kings, however, is not the actual secession from the Davidic kingdom but the subsequent building of alternative sanctuaries for pilgrimage and worship, in competition with the temple of Jerusalem. To understand this we need to return to the critical moment of Jereboam's revolt.

The unity of the tribes was always precarious, according to the history. The Book of Judges narrates times of crisis when some if not all the tribes allied to defeat a common enemy, but this was a temporary situation not a permanent one. After the death of Saul, we are told that the northern tribes approached David to rule over them, as well as his own tribe of Judah:

---

1. Translations of the Bible generally avoid the use of the name "Yahweh," replacing it with the title "the LORD" (in capitals). The translation used here is the New Revised Standard Version (NRSV).

2 Sam 5:1–5

1. Then all the tribes of Israel came to David at Hebron, and said, "Look, we are your bone and flesh. 2. For some time, while Saul was king over us, it was you who led out Israel and brought it in. The LORD said to you: It is you who shall be shepherd of my people Israel, you who shall be ruler over Israel." 3. So all the elders of Israel came to the king at Hebron; and King David made a covenant with them at Hebron before the LORD, and they anointed David king over Israel. 4. David was thirty years old when he began to reign, and he reigned forty years. 5. At Hebron he reigned over Judah seven years and six months; and at Jerusalem he reigned over all Israel and Judah thirty-three years.

There are several things to notice in this passage. First, there is the chronological information. Actually, it is the accession formula again: the age of the king at his accession (thirty) and the length of his reign (forty years). But the numbers should give cause for hesitation. While it is not impossible that these figures should be accurate, they do appear too good to be true: A reign of forty years fits the pattern of the history, and the total years of David's life add up to seventy, another symbolic number. Be that as it may, here we can see a distinction made between David's rule over Judah from Hebron and his rule over Israel from Jerusalem. That is, David was already king over the smaller area in the south before he was invited to become ruler over the northern tribes as well. The later split of the kingdom is a return to its earlier configuration, rather than a completely new division.

The history reflects this reality in recounting what happened after Solomon's death. According to the narrative, there was already unrest among the northern tribes led by Jeroboam, who went into exile in Egypt. When Solomon's son, Rehoboam, succeeded his father, he went to the northern city of Shechem expecting ratification of his rule. The northern tribes, however, were not so willing. The narrative points to a separate accession ceremony in the north, as there had been for David. The Israel of the following passage consists of the northern tribes, not the united nation.

1 Kgs 12:1–4, 13–17, 20

1. Rehoboam went to Shechem, for all Israel had come to Shechem to make him king. 2. When Jeroboam son of Nebat heard of it (for he was still in Egypt, where he had fled from King Solomon), then Jeroboam returned from Egypt. 3. And they sent and called him; and Jeroboam and all the assembly of Israel came and said to Rehoboam, 4. "Your father made our yoke heavy. Now therefore lighten the hard service of your father and his heavy yoke that he placed on us, and we will serve you."

13. The king answered the people harshly. He disregarded the advice that the older men had given him 14. and spoke to them according to the advice of the young men, "My father made your yoke heavy, but I will add to your yoke; my father disciplined you with whips, but I will discipline you with scorpions."

16. When all Israel saw that the king would not listen to them, the people answered the king, "What share do we have in David? We have no inheritance in the son of Jesse. To your tents, O Israel! Look now to your own house, O David." So Israel went away to their tents. 17. But Rehoboam reigned over the Israelites who were living in the towns of Judah. 18. When King Rehoboam sent Adoram, who was taskmaster over the forced labor, all Israel stoned him to death. King Rehoboam then hurriedly mounted his chariot to flee to Jerusalem. 19. So Israel has been in rebellion against the house of David to this day. 20. When all Israel heard that Jeroboam had returned, they sent and called him to the assembly and

made him king over all Israel. There was no one who followed the house of David, except the tribe of Judah alone.

Here we have a dramatization of the secession of Israel from the united monarchy. The dramatization is realistic and possibly harbors a memory of actual events. According to the narrative, it is because of Solomon's heavy-handedness that the northern tribes are already hesitant about accepting Rehoboam, who only makes matters worse. Consequently, the northern tribes decide to secede. That, at least, is the political rationale for the division.

The historian, however, also has a theological rationale for the breakup of the kingdom which goes back to Solomon's reign: "So Solomon did what was evil in the sight of the LORD, and did not completely follow the LORD, as his father David had done" (1 Kgs 11:6). The context for this judgment is Solomon's acceptance of other deities and building sanctuaries for them. The problem is that Solomon has just built the temple in Jerusalem, which the historian believes must be the *only* legitimate holy place of worship. Concomitant with that is the belief that only one God is to be worshiped: Yahweh, the God of Israel. The result of Solomon's actions is the loss of the kingdom, with the exception of Judah, and that because of the faithfulness of David.

All this is explained in a speech of the prophet Ahijah to Jereboam, who would become the first king of the northern kingdom (1 Kgs 11:30–39). Ten tribes are to be torn from Solomon's kingdom and given to Jeroboam, because Solomon has turned to other gods. As Ahijah speaking on behalf of God says, Solomon "has not walked in my ways, doing what is right in my sight and keeping my statutes and my ordinances, as his father David did" (11:33). Yet all is not lost; Ahijah continues: "Nevertheless I will not take the whole kingdom away from him but will make him ruler all the days of his life, for the sake of my servant David whom I chose and who did keep my commandments and my statutes" (11:34). Thus, in spite of Solomon's infidelity, the kingdom of Judah will continue "for the sake of my servant David."

When the Deuteronomistic historian looks back to find a reason for the division of the kingdom, he finds it in Solomon's infidelity to the exclusive worship of Israel's God. Yes, there is the political impetus of Solomon's and Rehoboam's heavy rule, but ultimately the cause lies with God. Similarly, the fact of Judah's continued existence points to God's continued protection. Since this blessing cannot be attributed to Solomon, it can only be due to David's loyalty. Thus the facts, as the Deuteronomist interprets them, have a logical cause. This is typical of ancient thinking that there must be a divine causality behind the political events of the day. For the Deuteronomist, history cannot be written without taking the divine factor into account.

To put it another way, history is written looking back and trying to make sense of past events leading to present circumstances. The Deuteronomistic historian looks back to a golden era of a united monarchy and believes that this was God's doing. He then looks back to the reality of a divided kingdom, which must still be God's doing in some fashion. As the history progresses, the historian also has to account for the destruction of the northern kingdom and eventually for the fall and destruction of Jerusalem and Judah. If God has not protected the people from these calamities, how can one explain it except through the theological concept of sin?

The rise of the northern kingdom is attributed to divine disapproval of Solomon's attention to other gods: The ten tribes will be "torn" from the kingdom and given to Jeroboam (1 Kgs 11:9). Jeroboam is still in good standing with God. The actual division of the people is not Jeroboam's sin, but the result of Solomon's sinfulness. Jeroboam, however, goes a step further, deciding to establish two centers of worship in the north so that the people will not have to go south. He astutely recognizes that the Davidic monarchy will have a strong pull on the people if they continue to worship in Jerusalem. For Jeroboam, this is a logical political move. But for the Deuteronomist it is a decisive act of infidelity to God. This is the sin of Jeroboam (1 Kgs 11:30; 13:34).

It is most probable that the two centers at Dan and Bethel were not shrines to *other* gods; rather they seem to have been intended as alternate Yahweh-shrines. To the Deuteronomist, however, it amounts to the same thing. The tradition itself points to legitimate sanctuaries around the country for worship—at Shiloh and Shechem, for example. But once the Jerusalem temple has come into existence, the Deuteronomist is convinced there should be no others, and there should have been no others. In all likelihood, people actually continued to worship Israel's God at these places quite happily, including the northern shrines of Dan and Bethel. But to the historian looking back, the existence of alternate holy sites is the cause of the ultimate downfall of the nation.

Since the northern sanctuaries remained active until the destruction of Israel, the historian could make the assessment that every northern king continued the sin of Jeroboam; hence the assessment that each king "did what was evil in the sight of the LORD." When the historian reports that the Assyrian Empire finally took over the northern kingdom and transported the populace elsewhere, he has no hesitation in ascribing these events to the sinfulness of the people:

> This occurred because the people of Israel had sinned against the LORD their God, who had brought them up out of the land of Egypt from under the hand of Pharaoh king of Egypt....
>
> Therefore the LORD was very angry with Israel and removed them out of his sight; none was left but the tribe of Judah alone....
>
> The LORD rejected all the descendants of Israel; he punished them and gave them into the hand of plunderers, until he had banished them from his presence. When he had torn Israel from the house of David, they made Jeroboam son of Nebat king. Jeroboam drove Israel from following the LORD and made them commit great sin. The people of Israel continued in all the sins that Jeroboam committed; they did not depart from them until the LORD removed Israel out of his sight, as he had foretold through all his servants the prophets. So Israel was exiled from

their own land to Assyria until this day. (2 Kgs 17:7, 18, 20–23)

The theological assessment is consistent from the beginning of the divided kingdom to its end. It is this consistency of concept and language which has persuaded scholars that a single perspective has shaped the narrative of the Deuteronomistic History.

History as Assessment 2: The Kings of Judah

As we examine the regnal formulas of the kings of Judah, we see another pattern emerge in its turn. Several examples are given:

Now in the eighteenth year of King Jeroboam son of Nebat, Abijam began to reign over Judah. He reigned for three years in Jerusalem. His mother's name was Maacah daughter of Abishalom. He committed all the sins that his father did before him; his heart was not true to the LORD his God, like the heart of his father David. Nevertheless for David's sake the LORD his God gave him a lamp in Jerusalem, setting up his son after him, and establishing Jerusalem; because David did what was right in the sight of the LORD, and did not turn aside from anything that he commanded him all the days of his life, except in the matter of Uriah the Hittite. (1 Kgs 15:1–5)

In the twentieth year of King Jeroboam of Israel, Asa began to reign over Judah; he reigned forty-one years in Jerusalem. His mother's name was Maacah daughter of Abishalom. Asa did what was right in the sight of the LORD, as his father David had done. But the high places were not taken away. Nevertheless the heart of Asa was true to the LORD all his days. (1 Kgs 15:9–11, 14)

Jehoshaphat son of Asa began to reign over Judah in the fourth year of King Ahab of Israel. Jehoshaphat was thirty-five years old when he began to reign, and he reigned twenty-five years in Jerusalem. His mother's name was Azubah daughter of Shilhi. He walked in all the way of his father Asa; he did not turn aside from it, doing what was right in the sight of the LORD; yet the high places were not taken away, and the people still sacrificed and offered incense on the high places. (1 Kgs 22:41–43)

In the fifth year of King Joram son of Ahab of Israel, Jehoram son of King Jehoshaphat of Judah began to reign. He was thirty-two years old when he became king, and he reigned eight years in Jerusalem. He walked in the way of the kings of Israel, as the house of Ahab had done, for the daughter of Ahab was his wife. He did what was evil in the sight of the LORD. Yet the LORD would not destroy Judah, for the sake of his servant David, since he had promised to give a lamp to him and to his descendants forever. (2 Kgs 8:16–19)

Although the kings of Israel are uniformly condemned, the reverse is not true for the kings of Judah. Each is judged according to the standard of loyalty set by the historian, and that standard is David, the founder of the dynasty. For the most part, these kings "do what is right in the sight of the LORD," as opposed to the kings of Israel. The flaw is that they do not remove the "high places," alternate shrines of worship away from Jerusalem. But even when a king "does what is evil in the sight of the LORD," there is no threat of destruction for Judah. On the contrary, Judah will be preserved no matter what because of a promise made to David's house. This is expressed especially in the phrase concerning a lamp in Jerusalem, first expressed in the speech to Jeroboam by the prophet Ahijah, when he told of the coming division of the kingdom: "Yet to [Solomon's] son I will give one tribe, so that my servant David may always have a lamp before me in Jerusalem, the city where I have chosen to put my name" (1 Kgs 11:36). So all Judah's kings are evaluated by the example of the dynastic founder David, with the qualification that Judah will not be destroyed.

But there is more. The assurance of a "lamp" in Jerusalem is predicated on a prior promise to David himself. In the Deuteronomistic History, David is regarded as the paradigm for kingship; he alone is the king most faithful to the God of Israel. The temple is also central to Deuteronomistic theology, as the only legitimate site of worship and moreover appointed specifically by God to stand in Jerusalem. Yet the tradition holds that David did not build the temple. The history has to deal with this apparent contradiction and does so in 2 Sam 7, in the "oracle of Nathan." The narrative claims that David indeed intended to build a temple for God but was prevented by an oracle delivered by Nathan, David's court prophet. Playing on the word "house," Nathan declares that David will not build a house (temple) for God, but God will build a "house" or dynasty for David (2 Sam 7: 5, 11). Further, this house will last "forever":

> He shall build a house for my name, and I will establish the throne of his kingdom forever. I will be a father to him, and he shall be a son to me. When he commits iniquity, I will punish him with a rod such as mortals use, with blows inflicted by human beings. But I will not take my steadfast love from him, as I took it from Saul, whom I put away from before you. Your house and your kingdom shall be made sure forever before me; your throne shall be established forever. (2 Sam 7:13–16)

The Deuteronomistic interpretation of history can readily be seen here. Solomon's "sin" is already foreknown and there will be a punishment in human terms, that is, in political terms as the kingdom is divided. But since Judah remained as a kingdom, it must have seemed to the historian that the Davidic dynasty was indeed eternal; it had already survived over three hundred years by the time of Josiah. The longevity of the dynasty, as we have already noted, is attributed to David's faithfulness to Yahweh's service (1 Kgs 11:34).

Model Kings

Two kings of Judah are singled out for exceptional praise, Hezekiah and Josiah. Both of these kings are credited with religious reform, asserting the uniqueness of Yahweh-worship and the Jerusalem temple, high priorities for the Deuteronomistic ideal.

> In the third year of King Hoshea son of Elah of Israel, Hezekiah son of King Ahaz of Judah began to reign. He was twenty-five years old when he began to reign; he reigned twenty-nine years in Jerusalem. His mother's name was Abi daughter of Zechariah. He did what was right in the sight of the LORD just as his ancestor David had done. He removed the high places, broke down the pillars, and cut down the sacred pole. He broke in pieces the bronze serpent that Moses had made, for until those days the people of Israel had made offerings to it; it was called Nehushtan. He trusted in the LORD the God of Israel; so that there was no one like him among all the kings of Judah after him, or among those who were before him. (2 Kgs 18:1–5)

> Josiah was eight years old when he began to reign, he reigned thirty-one years in Jerusalem. His mother's name was Jedidah daughter of Adaiah of Bozkath. He did what was right in the sight of the LORD, and walked in all the way of his father David; he did not turn aside to the right or to the left....
>
> Moreover Josiah put away the mediums, wizards, teraphim, idols, and all the abominations that were seen in the land of Judah and in Jerusalem, so that he established the words of the law that were written in the book that the priest Hilkiah had found in the house of the LORD. Before him there was no king like him, who turned to the LORD with all his heart, with all his soul, and with all his might, according to all the law of Moses; nor did any like him arise after him. (2 Kgs 22:1–2; 23:24–25)

Both Hezekiah and Josiah are said to be unlike any king before or after, which is perhaps simply a way of expressing the highest praise. Both kings also carried out reforms of the worship of Israel's God emphasizing the centrality of the Jerusalem temple, which is the basis for their high assessment. The language, however, hearkens back to Deuteronomy. Josiah's devotion to God is expressed in exactly the words of Deuteronomy 6:5: "You shall love the LORD your God with all your heart, and with all your soul, and with all your might." Hezekiah treats the high places as Deuteronomy directs: "break down their altars, smash their pillars, hew down their sacred poles, and burn their idols with fire" (7:5).

Hezekiah is also credited for the retreat of the invading Assyrian forces, not by military strength but by faith in the God of Israel (2 Kgs 18:13–19:37). The dramatic reconstruction of the siege of Jerusalem includes the taunts of the enemy general Rabshakeh, who calls on the inhabitants of Jerusalem not to listen to Hezekiah nor, more tellingly, not to trust in Yahweh (vv. 28–30). Rabshakeh says they should instead trust in the king of Assyria, who will give them a land of grain and wine, of oil and honey, so that they will "live and not die" (v. 32). All this, of course, is what God has promised through the covenant. Led by Hezekiah, the people do not respond. The narrative includes an oracle by the prophet Isaiah and a promise of deliverance from the Assyrians. The Assyrians do break off the siege, apparently struck by plague, interpreted as sent by God.

Although the historian has dramatized events, the reconstruction is based on good evidence. Assyrian documents record the campaigns in Syria-Palestine in which Israel was conquered and its population deported, and Judah attacked. There is no record of Assyria's abandonment of the siege of Jerusalem but that is not surprising, since royal annals tended to overlook any setbacks. So the basic outline is accurate. The attribution of victory to Yahweh is also to be expected; victories were routinely attributed to national gods and this success would have both vindicated trust in Israel's God and boosted any religious reforms of Hezekiah. There is no reason to doubt the essential elements of the siege of Jerusalem although we have to remember that the details come from the dramatization.

King Josiah especially is held up for admiration in typically Deuteronomistic terms, doing "what was right in the sight of the LORD," following the path of David and not turning aside "to right or left" (cf. Deut 17:20). Not only that, he is credited with restoring the book of the law, holding a covenant ceremony and ensuring that its requirements were fulfilled (2 Kgs 22–23). Since the book of the law was probably an early version of the Book of Deuteronomy, it is no wonder that Josiah stands high in the estimation of the Deuteronomistic historian.

Josiah's reform is described in detail, although again dramatized in story form. The elements fit the Deuteronomistic program perfectly. In fact, it helps to have the text of Deuteronomy's "law of the king" to hand when reading of Josiah's actions:

> When he has taken the throne of his kingdom, he shall have a copy of this law written for him in the presence of the levitical priests. It shall remain with him and he shall read in it all the days of his life, so that he may learn to fear the LORD his God, diligently observing all the words of this law and these statutes, neither exalting himself above other members of the community nor turning aside from the commandment, either to the right or to the left, so that he and his descendants may reign long over his kingdom in Israel. (Deut 17:18–20)

Josiah undertakes renovation work on the temple during which a book is discovered and brought to the king. When Josiah hears the content of the book, he is concerned and sends for prophetic confirmation of the book's authenticity (2 Kgs 22). Subsequently, the king arranges for a public proclamation of the book and makes a covenant with God on behalf of the people, thus initiating the religious reform.

The king removes from Yahweh-worship everything that the Deuteronomistic theology deems alien: The temple is cleared of various objects sacred to other gods such as Baal and Asherah; alternate places of worship are closed down and their priests brought into Jerusalem, although in a lesser capacity; horses and chariots dedicated to the sun god (by previous kings of Judah!) are removed (2 Kgs 22:1–14). Other popular avenues to dealing with the divine world through soothsayers, mediums, and the like are also abolished (2 Kgs 23:24; cf. Deut 19:10–13). This is a fullscale reform of worship at the Jerusalem temple.

Josiah is also credited with destroying the alternate sanctuaries in Bethel and elsewhere in the north (2 Kgs 22:15–20). Finally, the king orders a celebration of passover:

> No such passover had been kept since the days of the judges who judged Israel, or during all the days of the kings of Israel or of the kings of Judah; but in the eighteenth year of King Josiah this passover was kept to the LORD in Jerusalem. (2 Kgs 23:21–23)

Everything has been done according to the Deuteronomistic vision (see especially Deut 12:2–7; 17:18–20;18:6–8, 9–14).

The Deuteronomistic History has narrated its reconstruction of the people of Israel, has organized the kings of the divided monarchy into a parallel and interlocking schema, and has shown how on the one hand the northern kingdom fell because of its "sin," but on the other the southern kingdom has survived because of David. Josiah's reforms only prove the Deuteronomist right. Up to this point the history and its assessment work. Not long after Josiah's reign, however, Judah falls to the Babylonians, Jerusalem and its temple are destroyed. It is clear that a re-assessment is in order.

The Revised Edition

The details of Josiah's reform and its conformity to Deuteronomistic ideals have led many scholars to think that it was during his reign that the first and/or major edition of the history was completed. Further, the assessment of the Judahite kings implies that both the Davidic monarchy and the Jerusalem temple were still in existence. This part of the history must have been composed before the calamitous events of the Babylonian conquest. But the history continues to relate the shifting alliances and subsequent defeats suffered by Judah during the reigns of three of Josiah's sons, ending with Zedekiah. The Babylonians had already made one campaign into the region to regain control from the Egyptians, but during the reign of Zedekiah a second campaign was waged against Jerusalem. A second deportation of Jerusalemites took place while the walls of the city were destroyed and the temple stripped.

It is the material in the last two and a half chapters of Kings which suggests a second edition of the history. The Deuteronomistic ideology up to this point had depended on the stability of the Davidic dynasty and the security of Jerusalem and Judah. They had lasted, unlike the northern kingdom. The complete subservience of Judah, the removal and replacement of its kings by outside forces and its ultimate downfall, culminating in the destruction of the temple, must have shattered the complacency of that vision. The revised version of the history brings the narrative up-to-date but must deal with unpalatable facts—the loss of Judah and Jerusalem—and must also provide a reason for this turn of events. Just as the downfall of the northern kingdom was understood to be the result of sin, similarly sin must have caused the fall of Judah and Jerusalem with its temple.

The history had already set out the kings of Judah as more or less faithful to Yahweh, but saved by the promise to David of a lasting dynasty and presence in Jerusalem no matter how attenuated. What could have worked to break that commitment? The answer for the Deuteronomist lies in the reign of Josiah's grandfather, Manasseh. The son of Hezekiah, the only king besides Josiah to receive highest praise from the historian, Manasseh apparently did not follow in his father's footsteps. On the contrary, he is depicted as reversing his father's religious reforms, bringing back all the rites and symbols so hated by the Deuteronomist (2 Kgs 21:1–9). While this king is said to have ruled for fifty-five years, nothing else is recorded of him in this history—nothing else matters. It is precisely this kind

of silence about a lengthy and presumably stable reign that emphasizes the agenda of the historian. The warning of disaster to come is
attributed rather vaguely to "the prophets" without further specifica-
tion (2 Kgs 21:10). Manasseh's sinfulness is so great that it will over-
ride the promise of the permanence of the temple in Jerusalem, and
the city will suffer the same fate as the north (21:13–14). Not even
Josiah's reforms will avert this catastrophe.

A reminder of Manasseh's responsibility for the fall of Judah
turns up in the middle of Josiah's regnal formula:

> Before him there was no king like him, who turned to the
> LORD with all his heart, with all his soul, and with all his
> might, according to the law of Moses; nor did any like
> him arise after him. *Still the LORD did not turn from the*
> *fierceness of his great wrath, by which his anger was kindled*
> *against Judah, because of all the provocations with which*
> *Manasseh had provoked him. The LORD said, "I will remove*
> *Judah also out of my sight, as I have removed Israel; and I*
> *will reject this city that I have chosen, Jerusalem, and the*
> *house of which I said, My name shall be here."* Now the rest
> of the acts of Josiah and all that he did, are they not writ-
> ten in the Book of the Annals of the Kings of Judah? (2
> Kgs 23:25–28)

The usual regnal formula has been interrupted by the comment on
Manasseh and suggests that a later hand has inserted the comment
in light of subsequent events. Without the reference to Manasseh,
Josiah's formula reads smoothly and on a high note. With the reference to Manasseh, a jarring element has been introduced to "put a
spin" on Josiah's reign: All his accomplishments were not enough to
counteract Manasseh's wickedness. Scholars take note of such
apparent intrusions in the text, which suggest secondary editing or
revising.

The first version of the history is generally understood by scholars to have come from the time of Josiah, while the present and future
still looked rosy; the second edition must have appeared after the

events described, that is, after the end of the monarchy and the onset
of the exile.[2] Thus we can speak of a pre-exilic or Josianic edition of
the history and an exilic edition. In both editions, a similar theology is
operative and so it is assumed that both versions originate in a single
intellectual context, the Deuteronomistic school of thought, associated with those who advocated worship of Yahweh alone.

The Deuteronomistic History is permeated with the belief that
God intervenes in human history. This is a given not only in the biblical texts but in the ancient worldview. The divine sphere is operative constantly; nothing happens in the realm of humans that has not
been ordained in the heavens. This is true of ancient Egypt, Assyria,
Babylonia, as well as ancient Israel. It is not surprising, then, that
the historian would evaluate the kings of Israel and Judah according
to a religious perspective.

History in the Books of Kings

What does the history consist of in the books of Kings? A brief
consideration of the content reveals what kind of history this is: It
deals with great events, with the actions of kings and prophets, so it
is political rather than social history. There is a chronological framework, including the regular accession formulas and death notices for
each king. There are stories of public figures rather than private individuals and of events which have impact on the entire nation. Even
the prophets are those who interact with kings and try to influence
policy: court prophets such as Nathan and Isaiah, prophets who cri-
tique the monarchy such as Elijah and Elisha.

Although the historian makes reference to the Annals of the
Kings of Israel and Judah, it appears that he has been very selective in
what he includes in the overall narrative. Some campaigns and building projects are not deemed significant enough for further development (for example, 1 Kgs 22:45). The account of the reign of Abijam

---

2. Some scholars posit an earlier version dating from the time of Hezekiah, king of
Judah at the time of the fall of the northern kingdom, Israel.

of Judah is almost entirely formulaic, except for a statement that the war against Jeroboam was continued (1 Kgs 15:1–8). Abijam's son Asa is said to have reigned for forty-one years. The account of his reign consists of some details of religious reform and a story of how he got the king of Aram to change sides in the long-standing war with the north. Apparently he also undertook some building projects, but otherwise nothing more is narrated of his long reign (1 Kgs 15:9–24). Yet Asa emerges as a true defender of Judah on the basis of these brief highlights, the most significant according to the historian.

When we stop to think about it, we are given only summaries and highlights from each king's reign, not a comprehensive treatment. This is no doubt because the history is an overview of major trends. But how does the historian decide what is significant? In the regnal formulas, what is consistent is a statement about the king's attitude toward public religion, whether or not he followed the way of Jereboam in the north or David in the south. This is the criterion for both the assessment of the king and for the inclusion of illustrative materials. Recognizing that the criterion is religious rather than political alerts us to the kind of history we are reading: It is not an objective appraisal of the rulers of Judah and Israel but rather a judgment on the kings (and people) who by and large have not been faithful to God's law. Any strictly historical data (in the modern sense) are secondary in importance. While the historical framework is important to the historian, the material included varies in historical value while remaining consistent in theological perspective.

Josiah's reform, inspired by the vision of the uniqueness of Judah's God and the exclusivity of temple worship, was the benchmark for the historian looking back at what he knew of Israel's history. Modern historians regard Josiah's reform as the culmination of a move toward worship of Yahweh alone, but from the perspective of the Deuteronomist it was a return to the original purity intended by God. The stability of the Davidic monarchy and its permanent residence in Jerusalem only confirmed that point of view, at least until the fall of the kingdom of Judah. And even then, the theology undergoes a refinement rather than a complete overhaul.

For Further Reading

Robert B. Coote and Mary P. Coote, *Power, Politics, and the Making of the Bible* (Minneapolis: Fortress Press, 1990), Chapters 5–7.

Herschel Shanks, ed., *Ancient Israel: From Abraham to the Roman Destruction of the Temple* (Upper Saddle River, NJ: Prentice Hall/ Biblical Archaeology Society, 1999), Chapter 4, "The United Monarchy," especially pp. 106–108, and Chapter 5, "The Divided Monarchy."

J. Glen Taylor, "Was Yahweh Worshiped as the Sun?" *Biblical Archaeology Review* 24/4 (May/June 1994), 52–61, 90–91.

For Further Study

1. Today scholars point out that the actual religious situation up to the time of Josiah was more complex than the biblical picture suggests. Research the archaeological findings that shed light on religious practices in Israel and Judah during the monarchy.

2. Read 2 Sam 7 more closely. If speeches reveal the author's interpretation of events, how do Nathan's prophecy and David's prayer reveal the Deuteronomist's theology?

3. Read 1 Kgs 11:26–40 and compare with 2 Sam 7:1–17. What is the historian's position on Jereboam's political claim on the northern kingdom? To what extent can Jereboam be compared with David in their accession to kingship?

4. The Book of Chronicles covers much the same material as the Deuteronomistic History, but with alternative interpretations. Compare 1 Chron 15:25–16:3 with 2 Sam 6:12–23, and/or 2 Chron 9:22–31 with 1 Kgs 10:26–11:41. What differences are there and for what purpose? (Many other texts can be compared; see the cross references in the relevant books.)

11

"In Those Days
There Was No King in Israel":
The Books of Joshua and Judges

The Deuteronomistic History runs from Joshua and Judges through 1 and 2 Samuel to Kings. Whereas Kings is relatively easy to understand as a history with its regnal formulas and chronology, Joshua and Judges look different. They deal with the pre-monarchic period, reconstructing Israel's hazy past. In this chapter we shall take a brief look at these two books to situate them in the history and to see how the historian works with a scarcity of archival material.

The Book of Joshua and the Language of War

One major difference between the Book of Joshua and the books of Kings is a lack of chronological framework. We are given some indication of time through the person of Caleb. After the Israelites have taken over Canaan and are being allotted land, Caleb comments that it is now forty-five years since he was sent by Moses to scout out the new land (Josh 14:7–10; Num 13). Forty of those years were spent in the wilderness, so it can be concluded that settlement in the land has taken five years. The Book of Joshua depicts the entrance into the land of Canaan as a swift military campaign of conquest and acquisition. More than that, it is an action of total annihilation of the local inhabitants, quite disturbing to the modern reader, and one commanded by God:

So Joshua defeated the whole land, the hill country and the Negeb and the lowland and the slopes, and all their kings; he left no one remaining, but utterly destroyed all that breathed, as the LORD God of Israel commanded. (Josh10:40)

In order to understand this text and the tenor of the Book of Joshua, we have to return to the Book of Deuteronomy.

As we saw with the assessment of the kings, the book of Deuteronomy contains the theology which informs the history. Through the speeches of Moses, Deuteronomy looks forward to a time when the Israelites will take possession of the land of Canaan. But Canaan is already inhabited, so the program of settlement will have to include their removal. Since they are "alien" peoples who worship gods other than Israel's own God, Yahweh, and thus pose a threat to exclusive Yahweh-worship, they must be eliminated.

Deut 7:1–6

When the LORD your God brings you into the land that you are about to enter and occupy, and he clears away many nations before you—the Hittites, the Girgashites, the Amorites, the Canaanites, the Perizzites, the Hivites, and the Jebusites, seven nations mightier and more numerous than you—2. and when the LORD your God gives them over to you and you defeat them, then you must utterly destroy them. Make no covenant with them and show them no mercy. 3. Do not intermarry with them, giving your daughters to their sons or taking their daughters for your sons, 4. for that would turn away your children from following me, to serve other gods. Then the anger of the LORD would be kindled against you, and he would destroy you quickly. 5. But this is how you must deal with them: break down their altars, smash their pillars, hew down their sacred poles, and burn their idols with fire. 6. For you are a people holy to the LORD your God; the LORD your God has chosen you out of all the peoples on earth to be his people, his treasured possession.

The account of the Israelite conquest of Canaan in the Book of Joshua is shaped by this passage of Deuteronomy. Archaeological investigation has revealed that there is no evidence of a military takeover of Canaan as described in Joshua, a factor that the modern reader will have to take into account. Rather, the settlement of Israelites seems to have been a gradual spreading out of the population in the hill country. What then is going on in the history? The book of Joshua provides a reconstruction of events, based not on evidence—which could not have been available to the historian several hundred years later—but on a theology of right worship of God. The people of Israel must worship their God exclusively and eschew other gods, which in any case belong to other peoples. In order to keep Israel from contact with such gods, the land must be cleared of all "contamination."

This is clearly rhetorical language and has its own internal logic: The history was written when worship of Yahweh-alone was beginning to emerge among the Israelites. The language of war is strong, excessive to the modern ear, but underlines the importance of exclusive worship of Israel's God. It also belongs in a culture that understood war and conquest, and the custom of kings to impose their own gods on conquered groups. The main difference between the Deuteronomistic idea of conquest and that of surrounding nations is the emphasis on exclusivity and intolerance for other gods. Thus the historian imbued with the theology of Deuteronomy sees Israel as a conquering force which will wipe out any vestige of alien worship, leaving the field clear. Logically, if God gave the land to Israel, the other nations must have been dispossessed and this must have been accomplished by war (how else?); therefore the acquisition of the land must have been by military conquest. Conquest must have been swift and comprehensive, since this was Yahweh's war after all. If other gods belong to other nations, those nations must have been destroyed so that Israel could start with a clean slate. Thus Deuteronomy's admonition and the Book of Joshua's reconstruction of what must have happened, based on this theological understanding.

The language is typically Deuteronomistic and even formulaic, occurring repeatedly throughout the history. Verse 5, for example, is the program for Josiah's reforms. Israel's God is unique and must be seen to be so, not only in the exclusivity of the Jerusalem temple (at the time of the initial writing of the history) but through the people Israel as well. They are to be holy, that is, separated out from other nations and dedicated to Yahweh-alone. This is why intermarriage with other ethnic groups is forbidden (at least ideally) and ultimately why they have to be destroyed (again, at least in theory). Real life does not and did not match the theory.

Since the conquest is God's doing, then although Israel must go out to fight, it is God who achieves the victory. It is not surprising, then, that the first military exploit once the Israelites have crossed over into Canaan is the capture of Jericho, whose walls are miraculously breached when the sacred trumpets sound and the people shout—not by any military action of Israel (Josh 6:20)! Almost immediately comes the story of the non-conquest of Ai. The Israelite attack on Ai is thwarted by the disobedience of one man, Achan, who kept some booty for himself instead of dedicating it to God. Achan's disobedience led to the defeat of the Israelites and his punishment freed the Israelites to take the city of Ai. Thus the lesson is laid out: Obey God and Joshua and you will have success; disobey and the result will be disaster. Throughout the history, but especially in Joshua-Judges, this pattern is repeated.

The *Herem*: Sanctified by Destruction

Very quickly the conquest continues; the Israelites move through the entire land taking it over as if with no resistance. Once again, the language patterns are significant.

Josh 10:28–43

28. Joshua took Makkedah on that day, and struck it and its king with the edge of the sword; he utterly destroyed every person in it; he left no one remaining. And he did to the king of Makkedah as he had done to the king of Jericho.

29. Then Joshua passed on from Makkedah, and all Israel with him, to Libnah, and fought against Libnah. 30. The LORD gave it also and its king into the hand of Israel; and he struck it with the edge of the sword, and every person in it; he left no one remaining in it; and he did to its king as he had done to the king of Jericho.

31. Next Joshua passed on from Libnah, and all Israel with him, to Lachish, and laid siege to it, and assaulted it. 32. The LORD gave Lachish into the hand of Israel, and he took it on the second day, and struck it with the edge of the sword, and every person in it, as he had done to Libnah. 33. Then King Horam of Gezer came up to help Lachish; and Joshua struck him and his people, leaving him no survivors.

34. From Lachish Joshua passed on with all Israel to Eglon; and they laid siege to it, and assaulted it; 35. and they took it that day, and struck it with the edge of the sword; and every person in it he utterly destroyed that day, as he had done to Lachish.

36. Then Joshua went up with all Israel from Eglon to Hebron; they assaulted it, 37. and took it, and struck it with the edge of the sword, and its king and its towns, and every person in it; he left no one remaining, just as he had done to Eglon, and utterly destroyed it with every person in it.

38. Then Joshua, with all Israel, turned back to Debir and assaulted it, 39. and he took it with its king and all its

towns; they struck them with the edge of the sword, and utterly destroyed every person in it; he left no one remaining; just as he had done to Hebron, and, as he had done to Libnah and its king, so he did to Debir and its king.

40. So Joshua defeated the whole land, the hill country and the Negeb and the lowland and the slopes, and all their kings; he left no one remaining, but utterly destroyed all that breathed, as the LORD God of Israel commanded. 41. And Joshua defeated them from Kadesh-barnea to Gaza, and all the country of Goshen, as far as Gibeon. 42. Joshua took all these kings and their land at one time, because the LORD God of Israel fought for Israel. 43. Then Joshua returned, and all Israel with him, to the camp at Gilgal.

Although this is continuous text, it has been set out here to show that it is composed of a series of formulaic statements, not unlike the patterns we have already met in the books of Kings. The model is Jericho and the campaign proceeds methodically through the land until all is conquered. Certain key phrases are worth noting: "struck with the edge of the sword," "utterly destroyed," and "left no one remaining," and in fact some of the statements consist of little more than these phrases applied to a king and/or city. These phrases often occur together in describing the action of *herem*. This term, translated variously as "utterly destroyed" or "annihilated" on the one hand, or "devoted" or "put to the ban" on the other, means setting something (or someone) apart to be dedicated to God, and that is accomplished by destroying it. Such actions were taken by conquering kings not just in Israel. The famous inscription of King Mesha of Moab (part of modern Jordan) from the ninth century B.C.E. also speaks of "devoting" the inhabitants of Nebo to his god Chemosh in a ritual slaughter.

In the biblical concept of the *herem*, the total destruction of a city or nation is required because it has been dedicated or set aside for God. Once again, the direction is taken from Deuteronomy, which orders:

> But as for the towns of these peoples that the LORD your God is giving you as an inheritance, you must not let anything that breathes remain alive. You shall annihilate them—the Hittites and the Amorites, the Canaanites and the Perizzites, the Hivites and the Jebusites—just as the LORD your God has commanded, so that they may not teach you to do all the abhorrent things that they do for their gods, and you thus sin against the LORD your God. (Deut 20:16–18)

Here we see the rationale for this kind of war: fear of contamination in the worship of other gods. It bears repeating that Joshua's campaign is not a factual account. It is a retrojection of what must have happened given (a) God's complete control of events and (b) the evidence (at the time of the writing of the history) that the people do indeed worship other gods besides Yahweh. Thus, to the historian, the original exclusive worship of Yahweh must have been compromised—as indeed further stories indicate. It is a cry—a war cry—for total separation from others who do not worship rightly.

The two models are Jericho and Ai. If the Israelites obey God and their duly appointed leaders, then success will be theirs through divine intervention. If, however, they disobey the law, then disaster will strike. The lesson for readers of the history is not a military one but a moral one: obedience to God's law as set out in the Book of the Law discovered in the temple in Josiah's reign. The biblical writer even makes it clear that the conquest of Canaan did not follow the theory, the "ideal," in later comments in Joshua and especially in the first chapter of Judges.

The second half of Joshua is taken up with the allotment of land entitlements to the various tribes, including the delineation of boundaries (for example, 15:1–12). It ends with a renewal of the covenant and the death of Joshua (Chap. 24). Israel is faithful; all is well. Or is it? There are already hints that the conquest is not a total success. In the segment concerning the towns allocated to Judah we discover that "the people of Judah could not drive out the Jebusites, the inhabitants of Jerusalem; so the Jebusites live with the people of Judah in Jerusalem to this day" (15:63).[1] This passage also correlates with the later story that it was David who took Jerusalem, making it his own capital (2 Sam 5:6–10), but in the meantime it points to the incomplete conquest of the land. Similarly, the tribes of Ephraim and Manasseh are unable to drive out all the Canaanites (16:10; 17:12). Another hint appears at the very end of the book, when Joshua's death is narrated. There we read that "Israel served the LORD all the days of Joshua, and all the days of the elders who outlived Joshua and had known all the work that the LORD did for Israel" (24:31). While this seems a positive note to end on, there is the not-yet-formulated question "what happened in the next generation?" which the Book of Judges will answer.

The Book of Judges:
A Cycle of Oppression and Salvation

The Book of Judges continues the narrative of the conquest but with a different slant. The tribe of Judah does not drive out all the inhabitants from that territory (1:19), nor could the tribe of Manasseh drive out all the inhabitants from their territory (1:27). The same is true for Ephraim, Zebulun, Asher, and Naphthali (1:29, 30, 31, 33). The Danites are forced back into the hills (v. 34). According to Judges, then, the actual conquest has mixed results, which has the effect in the history of injecting a note of realism and

---

1. Confusingly, there are different versions of what happened to Jerusalem: According to Josh 15:63, the tribe of Judah was unable to drive out the Jebusites, who remained "to this day," while in Judg 1:21 it is the Benjaminites who cannot drive out the inhabitants. On the other hand, according to Judg 1:8 the tribe of Judah did take Jerusalem. In Judg 19:10-12, however, Jerusalem is still a Jebusite city. Add to this the account of David's capture of Jerusalem to see how difficult it is for the modern historian to find out "what really happened." The last account is probably closest to actual events, with the competing traditions in Joshua-Judges reflecting political "spin" by making certain claims for and against the tribes of Judah and Benjamin.

"correcting" the narrative of Joshua.[2] But the Book of Judges also has its own agenda.

Judges is shaped by another pattern that incorporates chronological material. There is a cyclical pattern to the narratives of Judges which appears to be furthering the movement forward while leaving Israel metaphorically stuck in the same place. There is no progress to this part of the history. The reason for this lies partly in the lack of available data to the historian who nonetheless wants to narrate what happened to Israel before the monarchy was established, and partly in the ideology of the history which looks forward to David and a united Israel. The historian collects, adapts, and composes stories about local heroes setting them in a broader context to create a "time of the judges," a reconstruction of the era before centralized government. There are no references to annals or records of any kind; there are only stories and a list of those who "judged Israel."

Judg 2:11–23

Then the Israelites did what was evil in the sight of the LORD and worshiped the Baals; 12. and they abandoned the LORD, the God of their ancestors, who had brought them out of the land of Egypt; they followed other gods, from among the gods of the peoples who were all around them, and bowed down to them; and they provoked the LORD to anger. 13. They abandoned the LORD, and worshiped Baal and the Astartes. 14. So the anger of the LORD was kindled against Israel, and he gave them over to plunderers who plundered them, and he sold them into the power of their enemies all around, so that they could no longer withstand their enemies. 15. Whenever they marched out, the hand of the LORD was against them to bring misfortune, as the LORD had warned them and sworn to them; and they were in great distress.

---

2. The presence of different interpretations of "what happened" is one of the reasons why modern scholars posit the likelihood of more than one edition of the history.

16. Then the LORD raised up judges, who delivered them out of the power of those who plundered them. 17. Yet they did not listen even to their judges; for they lusted after other gods and bowed down to them. They soon turned aside from the way in which their ancestors had walked, who had obeyed the commandments of the LORD; they did not follow their example.

18. Whenever the LORD raised up judges for them, the LORD was with the judge, and he delivered them from the hand of their enemies all the days of the judge; for the LORD would be moved to pity by their groaning because of those who persecuted and oppressed them. 19. But whenever the judge died, they would relapse and behave worse than their ancestors, following other gods, worshiping them and bowing down to them. They would not drop any of their practices or their stubborn ways. 20. So the anger of the LORD was kindled against Israel; and he said, "Because this people have transgressed my covenant that I commanded their ancestors, and have not obeyed my voice, 21. I will no longer drive out before them any of the nations that Joshua left when he died." 22. In order to test Israel, whether or not they would take care to walk in the way of the LORD as their ancestors did, 23. the LORD had left those nations, not driving them out at once, and had not handed them over to Joshua.

There are several things to notice in this passage. First, it deals with a recurrent situation rather than one discrete event: "whenever they marched out…, whenever the LORD raised up judges…, whenever the judge died…." This is the language of repetition and generality so there are no specifics provided. The author is establishing the pattern which will shape the Book of Judges. Secondly, we are told that the Israelites violated the covenant by worshiping alien gods, thus rousing God's anger. And finally, we note the very language, typical of the Deuteronomistic History: "abandoning the

LORD," "doing evil in the sight of the LORD," "kindling the anger of the LORD."

Also significant is the last statement, which contradicts the conquest account of Joshua and moreover attributes the lack of success to the sinfulness of the people. Again, the historian had to deal with the reality that other groups besides Israel were living in the land. How could this be, if the "conquest" was to have cleared the land of these peoples? It could not have been because of Joshua, appointed by God to succeed Moses (Deut 31:14, 23); nor apparently of the first generation in the land, who remained faithful (Josh 24:31). One answer to the problem is to attribute Joshua's lack of total success to God's decision to "test" Israel (v. 22). But the continuing presence of the other peoples must have meant that Israel failed the test—repeatedly. Or, to put it another way, since people in the land continued to worship a variety of gods even at the time of Josiah's reform, Israel must have been lacking in fidelity all along. And yet Yahweh-worship was still strong, so there must also have been a degree of fidelity. Modern historians point to the complexity of actual religious practices in the land during the period of the monarchy and beyond. But to the ancient Deuteronomist, plurality pointed to a failure to keep Yahweh-worship pure and exclusive. Thus the pattern of fidelity and apostasy.

The problem therefore must have continued with successive generations. Notice how the writer lays it out:

> Israel served the LORD all the days of Joshua, and all the days of the elders who outlived Joshua and had known all the work that the LORD did for Israel. (Josh 24:31)

> When Joshua dismissed the people, the Israelites all went to their own inheritances to take possession of the land. The people worshiped the LORD all the days of Joshua, and all the days of the elders who outlived Joshua, who had seen all the great work that the LORD had done for Israel. Joshua son of Nun, the servant of the LORD, died at the age of one hundred ten years. (Judg 2:6–8)

Moreover, that whole generation was gathered to their ancestors, and another generation grew up after them, who did not know the LORD or the work that he had done for Israel. Then the Israelites did what was evil in the sight of the LORD and worshiped the Baals…. (Judg 2:10–11)

Joshua's death is repeated at the beginning of Judges to remind the reader of the first generation in the land and to make a close connection between the end of that generation and the sinfulness of the next. Note the distinction between the two: The former generation "knew" what their God had done for Israel (they were born during the wilderness years, experiencing the effects of the exodus) whereas the next generation "did not know" the work of Yahweh. This would be true of every generation thereafter. Without direct knowledge of what Yahweh had done, the Israelites would always be inclined to turn to other gods, as in the historian's own time. What would save the people ultimately would be the book of the law. If we look at this from the perspective of the historian, we can understand the significance of the book of the law, both at the time of Josiah, because it led to religious reform, and later after Jerusalem's fall, because it contained God's teaching *(torah)*.

With the generation after Joshua, the pattern commences. The Israelites "do what is evil in the sight of the LORD," they are oppressed by their enemies, God raises up a savior, and the land is at rest for a time. The first example in the pattern is short (there are no stories attached to the hero) but all the elements are there.

Judg 3:7–11

The Israelites did what was evil in the sight of the LORD, forgetting the LORD their God, and worshiping the Baals and the Asherahs. 8. Therefore the anger of the LORD was kindled against Israel, and he sold them into the hand of King Cushan-rishathaim of Aram-naharaim; and the Israelites served Cushan-rishathaim eight years. 9. But when the Israelites cried out to the LORD, the LORD raised up a deliverer for the Israelites, who delivered them, Othniel son of Kenaz, Caleb's younger brother. 10. The spirit of the LORD came upon him, and he judged Israel; he went out to war, and the LORD gave King Cushan-rishathaim of Aram into his hand; and his hand prevailed over Cushan-rishathaim. 11. So the land had rest forty years. Then Othniel son of Kenaz died.

Not every hero story contains each element, but the pattern is quite consistent for Ehud (3:12–30; a "locked room" mystery!), Deborah (4:1–5:31), and Gideon (6:1–8:28). In each case the formula frames the beginning and end of each narrative. The first part of the formula appears before the stories of Jephthah (see 10:6–8) and Samson (13:1) but not the closing remark about rest in the land. On the other hand, as in the case of Othniel, the spirit of God comes upon Jephthah (11:29) and Samson (14:19; 15:14). The heroes are called "deliverers" or are said to have delivered Israel from the enemies (see also Shamgar, 3:31), or else they are said to have judged Israel, but not usually both.

Besides the stories of warrior heroes who deliver Israel, there is a list of "minor" judges preceding and following the story of Jephthah. Each appears with a brief notice of name and tribe and the length of time he judged Israel (10:1–5 and 12:8–15). Jephthah also appears in the list, the only one to have a story attached to his name. Samson is said to have judged Israel for twenty years (15:20; 16:31) but his stories strike an incongruous note, since he does not lead an army to battle but rather seems to terrorize the local population, until his final act of bravery which does destroy the Philistines. The concept continues into the first book of Samuel[3] where Eli the priest at Shiloh is said to have judged Israel forty years (1 Sam 4:18) and Samuel himself "judged Israel all the days of his life" (1 Sam

---

3. Although the history is divided into individual "books," probably related to the length of a scroll, the narrative itself is continuous from Judges into 1 Samuel. In modern Christian bibles, the Book of Ruth has been inserted and breaks the transition.

7:15). He is the last real judge and provides the transition to monarchy by anointing first Saul, who was later rejected by God, and then David, the greatest king in the eyes of the historian.

"In Those Days There Was No King in Israel"

The final chapters of Judges have a different formula framing the narratives: "In those days there was no king in Israel; all the people did what was right in their own eyes" (17:6). This seems to be a kind of mirror-image of the complaint that the Israelites did "what was evil in the sight of the LORD," and introduces stories not about heroes but about individuals who get caught up in dubious actions. The formula is partly repeated in 18:1 and 19:1, then in full at the very end of the book (21:25), and links two narratives in Chapters 17–18 and 19–21. Each of these narratives is complex and puzzling, and even shocking in the case of Chapter 19, the rape of the woman from Bethlehem. The different tone of these narratives has led most scholars to understand them as later additions, not part of even the revised edition of the Deuteronomistic History, but a few scholars have argued for their inclusion. Nonetheless, these chapters are difficult. For our present purposes, it is enough to note the presence of the narratives and to consider how they could fit into the overall history.

The narrative of Judg 17–18 concerns a certain Micah who with money apparently stolen from his mother sets up a shrine with sacred symbols including an idol (17:1–5). Now Micah's name (*mi- ka-yehu*) means "Who is like Yahweh?" yet he sets up another god! Micah also hires a Levite of Bethlehem of Judah as his priest, but the Levite gets an offer he cannot refuse from some bullying Danites, who steal both Micah's idol and the priest and establish a sanctuary at Dan. The Levite turns out to be a grandson of Moses (18:30). The second narrative in Judg 19–21 concerns another Levite with connections to Bethlehem, who while traveling with his wife through Jebusite (non-Israelite) territory seeks safe shelter in a Benjaminite village. No one offers them hospitality except a man from the northern tribe of Ephraim. The Levite's wife is raped by the Benjaminites in a story modeled on the account of Lot in Sodom (Gen 19). The unnamed wife dies, although how she dies and when is not entirely clear (Judg 19:27–29). The Levite summons "all Israel" to avenge this terrible deed. A war of retribution is waged by the Israelites against one of their own tribes, resulting in Benjamin's near annihilation.

The linking formula certainly fits the agenda of the history. It also points out from a negative perspective the need for a monarchy: when there is "no king in Israel," shrines are multiplied (Chapters 17–18) and tribes take on campaigns of retribution with disastrous results (19–21). In the last narrative, there is a distinct lack of leadership and consequent internecine war which a monarchy would have avoided. By the end of Judges, it is clear that a monarchy is needed, and so the stage is set for the story of Samuel and his role in setting a king over Israel. The narratives also contain foreshadowing of later events in the history. A holy site is established in Dan, later to be one of the idolatrous shrines of the northern kingdom. In Chapter 19, it is the tribe of Benjamin which is the root cause of the subsequent war; but the tribe of Benjamin is also the tribe of Saul, Israel's first king who was ultimately rejected by God for his lack of trust.

One final note: The Levite of Judg 17–18 is named as "Jonathan son of Gershom, son of Moses," which places him in that generation after Joshua and his contemporaries, who "did not know the LORD" (2:10). In the narrative of the Benjaminite war in Judg 19–21, we discover a certain "Phinehas son of Eleazar, son of Aaron" ministering before the ark of the covenant at Bethel (20:27–28). He, too, belongs to the same generation. In fact, Eleazar's death is noted just after Joshua's in Josh 24:33, the very end of the book. These two leaders were of the same generation after Moses and their deaths signal the start of the next generation, which Judges claims began the whole cycle of infidelity.

The Era of the Judges

In the account of Othniel, the model which begins the cyclical patten, the concept of a deliverer raised by God is associated with

160

the idea of "judging" Israel. A list of those who are said to have judged Israel in Chapters 10 and 12 is combined with stories of heroes who are said to have delivered Israel. The association seems to be the work of the writer who set up the pattern of oppression and deliverance. That is, the era of judges is a reconstruction of Israel's experience in the time before the monarchy. There is little factual support for the reconstructed version of events but even to the modern scholar it is overall a likely scenario, in that there must have been tribal leaders in local wars before the Israelites were unified into a kingdom. What the actual history was, we do not know, but the stories illustrate the Deuteronomistic notion that without a central sanctuary for worship of Yahweh, and without leadership, Israel was inclined to go to other gods. The great advantage of monarchy, especially in the person of David, was the establishment of a permanent succession of leadership centered around the Jerusalem temple of the God of Israel.

The Book of Joshua brings the people Israel into the land and establishes the boundaries of both the land and the regional zones of the tribes. It is a kind of charter to identify for later Israel where these tribal territories lie, and at the same time it is also a claim to the whole land. Further, the theology of Deuteronomy is reaffirmed and dramatized. The Book of Judges, however or more accurately the era of the judges in Judges and 1 Samuel—offers a more realistic and political assessment of the settlement of the land. It is a reconstruction of the presumed transitional stage between the legendary entrance into the land and the known monarchy. The historian has created the era out of stories of heroes and tribal battles and a traditional list of leaders, shaped by a framework constructed out of a theology of Israel's infidelity and God's deliverance.

We should not be surprised that Joshua and Judges are not accurate for this period of Israel's history. It would be unreasonable to expect the writer to have more than legends and names from so long before. Archives of any value would only have begun with the establishment of the monarchy, its capital, and its palace-temple complex. We can, however, admire the genius of the reconstruction, which makes so much sense when understood in its proper context.

For Further Reading

Robert B. Coote and Mary P. Coote, *Power, Politics, and the Making of the Bible* (Minneapolis: Fortress Press, 1990), Chapter 2.

Hershel Shanks, ed., *Ancient Israel: From Abraham to the Roman Destruction of the Temple* (Upper Saddle River, NJ: Prentice Hall/Biblical Archaeology Society, 1999), Chapter 3, "The Settlement in Canaan."

Frank Antony Spina, "Reversal of Fortune," *Bible Review* XVII/4 (August 2001), 24–30, 53–54 [Achan's sin at Ai].

Phyllis Trible, *Texts of Terror* (Philadelphia: Fortress Press, 1984), Chapter 3, "An Unnamed Woman: The Extravagance of Violence."

For Further Study

1. Read the story of Ai in Josh 7–8. Discuss the Deuteronomistic language and ideas in this narrative.

2. Read the list of "minor judges" in Judg 10:1–5 and 12:7–15. What pattern is discernible? How does the list compare with the regnal formulas of the kings (see the previous chapter)?

3. There are some intriguing stories of women in the Book of Judges. What are their roles? How do their stories affect our understanding of Israelite women and/or the biblical text? (This question can be approached in an overview or in a closer study of one narrative.)

12

HISTORY IN CONTEXT

The purpose of history is to explain the present—to say why the world around us is the way it is. History tells us what is important in our world, and how it came to be. It tells us why the things we value are the things we should value.

Michael Crichton, *Timeline*

That history is always compelling, and not only to academics, is readily witnessed by novels such as Michael Crichton's imaginative thriller *Timeline* or by the numerous documentaries available through television. So, too, is the Bible and its world perennially fascinating. People want to know "what happened"—again, witness the plethora of books and television documentaries. Even for those who do not have a religious commitment, the Bible is recognizable as a major shaping force in western culture, and the history it contains (or purports to contain) tells us modern North Americans something about our cultural origins. The Bible has helped to shape the world we know, has helped fashion our values.

Biblical studies have for over a century challenged a simplistic, literal, reading of biblical texts to open up new questions about the historicity of the people and events described therein. Archaeology has also both challenged and supported the picture of Israel's history presented in the Bible. Such studies reveal a much richer and more complex literature than we might at first imagine for such an ancient work. The biblical writers were more sophisticated than they often get credit for, and we see this in the historical writing as in other genres of biblical literature.

All history is a way of making sense of past events, connecting one event with another to create a coherent picture. In order to do this, each historian must choose a focus, which in turn dictates the limits of inquiry and requires the historian to choose which events to emphasize. More than that, however, the historian also interprets events in order to explain how they are interconnected. Sometimes the historian posits the motivations of key persons by analyzing and interpreting their actions. Thus, in addition to choice of material and interpretation there is also analysis and evaluation. All these characteristics are to be found in the biblical historians. Ancient histories are not entirely like modern histories, however.

The Idea of History

Our ideas of history owe their origins to the Greek writers Herodotus (c. 490–425 B.C.E.) and Thucydides (c. 454–399 B.C.E.). The very word *history*, in fact, comes from the Greek *historie*, "inquiry," which Herodotus used to describe his activity of collecting and assessing evidence. His is the earliest complete work that has come down to us, although there are fragments of other early attempts at history writing, and it is also the best example. Herodotus traveled widely, and included the sights and stories of other nations in his history. Importantly, he was more interested in human achievements than mythical heroic deeds. When he found alternative accounts in his inquiries, he included them all, leaving the reader to judge among them. Thucydides, a little later than Herodotus, was critical of his predecessors for being too willing to include "mythic" tales. He established the principle of making an impartial inquiry into past events and of inquiring into human actions, not those of the gods. By examining critically the information available to him, he hoped to discover the sequence of events that had brought the nation to its present condition. The historians, however, also aimed to instruct, to educate morally, and to entertain, that is, to make their histories interesting. So they and later historians used literary and rhetorical devices to shape their histories, especially in the speeches which they put in the mouths of the main historical characters. Thucydides, in spite of his claim to impartiality, was open about composing appropriate speeches for individuals and anonymous groups, and even paired speeches as a stylistic device. If Thucydides is the forerunner of modern ideas of history, Herodotus may be more significant for biblical historiography: Recent scholarship has renewed interest in the similarities of approach between Herodotus and biblical historical narratives.

The biblical historians shared with other ancient historians an interest in political rather than social history, viewed especially through the actions of great individuals. For the writers of 1 and 2 Maccabees, the primary focus was Judas Maccabeus, and later his brothers; for the author of Acts it was Peter for the first part of the book, followed by Paul in the second half. Although the Deuteronomistic History of the sixth century B.C.E. preceded the classical Greek historians by about a hundred years, we see a similar interest in great figures. In fact the history deals almost exclusively with the leaders of Israel from Joshua through the "judges" to Samuel, David, the kings, and prophets. Only those who truly led Israel in the ways of Yahweh have the approbation of the author. The earliest histories created coherent narratives from stories of outstanding individuals.

At the same time, ancient histories tend to be organized thematically, rather than strictly chronologically. This can be seen in Acts, which treats the development of the church geographically: first, in and around Jerusalem, then gradually moving outward. It can also be seen in 2 Maccabees, which structures the book around three attacks on the Jerusalem temple. The Deuteronomistic historian has also shaped the narrative with a focus on Jerusalem, centering on David and the establishment of the temple. Prior to Solomon, everything points towards the temple; afterwards, the kings are judged against the standard of David. The chronology is there, but it serves the theme rather than having priority.

Chronology was nonetheless important in ancient historiography. Early evidence for interest in chronology may be seen in genealogies and king lists in Mesopotamia, Egypt, and Greece, and also in the notion of "ages" in human history. We find some reference to the notion of "ages" in the Deuteronomistic History, which is divided into the "generation" of Joshua and his contemporaries, the time of the "judges," when "there was no king in Israel," and the period of the establishment of the temple, 480 years after the exodus. Luke-Acts has long been recognized as expressing three ages: the time before the Messiah up to and including John the Baptist, the period of Jesus' life, and the era of the Spirit narrated in Acts. The author of Luke-Acts is as specific as possible in dating the birth of Jesus and the appearance of John the Baptist. And of course the books of the Maccabees are filled with chronological detail.

Ancient Historiography as Moral Instruction

Within the narratives, we find the stories that give so much interest to the histories, yet are so dubiously historical. This is in keeping with the ancient model of providing typical episodes in the lives of the great persons. They have more to do with presenting the character of the person than with giving us accurate information. Any historical kernel will have to be discerned carefully. Here, too, belong the speeches, which are appropriate to the character and the audience but frequently give the historian's ideological position— what the character would have said in such circumstances. We can see this especially in the episode of Peter's vision and subsequent speech at Joppa in Acts 10, but also in the story of Solomon's judgment in 1 Kgs 3:16–28, which illustrates the king's famous wisdom, granted him in vv. 1–15. Similarly, the story of Mattathias's resistance in 1 Macc 2:15–28 illustrates both his courage and his theological motivation.

In all this, the ancient historians had no hesitation in making not only critical assessments of a person or era, but also moral judgments. This is as true of the secular historians as it is of the biblical historians. We have seen ample evidence of this kind of evaluation in the Deuteronomistic History, but it is also found in the other books. In 2 Maccabees particularly, the epitomist details the dreadful consequences of opposing God in the death of Antiochus (9:5–10) and of Nicanor (15:28–36). Acts, too, clearly evaluates actions against the author's ecclesiology in 5:1–11, the disconcerting story of Ananias and Sapphira, who are struck dead for their dishonesty. Once we recognize these dramatic representations, the author's theology becomes clearer, on the one hand, and on the other we as readers are freed of literal interpretations which cause more problems than they solve.

The language of biblical history writing is shaped in such a way as to anticipate and create a certain desired response. There is a common theme in all the historical books: the acknowledgment of the God of Israel and God's activity in human affairs. The theological slant of these writings is both clear and unapologetic; it is their purpose, their *raison d'être*. They are addressed to fellow believers to affirm and record divine activity in the history of the people of God. But they are not theological treatises or sermons, such as the Book of Qohelet (Ecclesiastes) or the Epistle to the Hebrews. They are historical in form and intent. They include documentation such as letters, references to annals, and chronological information, no matter what we may now judge of their historicity. Just as other histories narrated the story of this or that nation, so too do the biblical writers, but theirs is the story of the people of God, as they understood themselves to be. That perception informs the biblical histories, and to that extent they would not have agreed with Thucydides to leave the divine element out.

What about Historical Sources?

A major difficulty in dealing with ancient history is partly the paucity of evidence of the kind modern historians want, and partly the type of evidence that is available. For the period of the early church, one would expect there to be ample evidence since there were Roman writers, including historians, in abundance. The problem is that they were not particularly interested in a small group of sectarians deriving from the province of Judaea. Only the person we call Luke undertook to write an account of the earliest days of this community, showing how they spread out from their origins in Jerusalem to various sites in the Roman Empire. As we have seen, his resources were limited; if the scholars are correct, he did not even have copies of Paul's letters. He did have geographical locations of Christian communities, he had names of leading figures and some stories about them.

The author of 1 Maccabees was apparently able to draw on official sources, including correspondence and perhaps copies of treaties. The epitomist of 2 Maccabees, or perhaps the original author, did not have such ready access but drew also on legendary tales of martyrs. Between them they provide an identifiable and probable history of the end of the Seleucid rule and the beginning of the Hasmonean period. They also, as did Luke, had other histories to provide models and principles of history writing. In this respect, comparisons with other historians are very fruitful for understanding the style of the biblical writers. Josephus, a first century Jewish historian, is particularly helpful in understanding Luke. Josephus, himself an eyewitness and even participant in the most recent events he recorded, illustrates the flexibility an ancient writer had. He is quite capable of giving two versions of an event, or two different speeches by the same speaker on the same occasion, in order to get his point across. This having been said, however, both Luke and the writers of 1 and 2 Maccabees draw more on their familiarity with the First Testament books than on secular historians.

This brings us to the Deuteronomistic History, which does not have contemporary parallels. It is generally recognized that although traditions may go back much further, a connected narrative tracing the story of the people was composed around the beginning of the sixth century B.C.E. in educated circles in Jerusalem. The author(s) made use of lists, stories, poems, and other materials to create a sequential narrative, tracing the people's story from the (supposed) entrance into the land to "the present" (probably the time of King Josiah). The purpose was to show how obedience to Yahweh's commandments meant peace and security in the land, while disloyalty led to disunity and dispossession. The fall of the northern kingdom, Israel, provided evidence to support this position. Impartiality or objectivity was irrelevant, since the aim was to instruct Yahweh's people in loyalty.

Some few scholars have suggested that the history belongs to another period, closer to the time of Herodotus perhaps, or even later. But the majority still place this work, or the bulk of it, in the sixth century. What did this history draw on for models or precursors? The empires of Egypt and Mesopotamia (Assyria, Babylonia) did not apparently have this type of history writing although they were certainly interested in recording the deeds of the kings and other events. The origins of historiography in the ancient Near East lie in such records, in annals and chronicles, perhaps of the sort referred to in the Deuteronomistic History (see, for example, 1 Kgs 14:29). Besides king lists and genealogies, there were also royal inscriptions which sometimes were in narrative form: an incipient history. There were stories of the gods and heroes (for example, the epic of *Gilgamesh*) but not a full-scale history of a people.

History as the Story of a People

Herodotus and Thucydides understood history not as an epic of heroic struggles in a mythical past, but as the story of a people, a nation to use a modern term, in a realistic past, which provides a sense of identity. It informs its readers about where they have come from, how they are interconnected, what unifies them—what, in short, makes them an identifiable people. The biblical historians had a similar understanding. The Deuteronomistic History addressed the questions of identity and unity in the context of the Israelites and their land. So, too, do the books of Maccabees at a time when Judea was again a fledgling nation, this time struggling in a world of Seleucid control. And in a different context the author of Acts tells the "new" Israel, the Christian community, of its origins and identifying characteristics, as they established themselves in a Roman environment.

As we draw near to the close of this book, we realize that we are only at the beginning of the journey. Here we have examined a few texts from the historical books while leaving so many more unexplored. As historiography, the biblical books cannot be assessed against modern standards of accuracy, evidence, and impartiality, but they can be assessed against the standards of their own eras. In that context, the biblical histories stand up well. The more we read them in their own literary and historical contexts, the more we realize their creativity and integrity, their complexity and richness.

For Further Reading

Translations of the ancient historians Herodotus, Thucydides, and Josephus can be found in Penguin Classics and the Loeb Classical Library series.

Colin Hemer, *The Book of Acts in the Setting of Hellenistic History* (Winona Lake, IN: Eisenbrauns, 1990), Chapter 3, "Ancient Historiography."

Steve Mason, *Josephus and the New Testament* (Peabody, MA: Hendrickson, 1992).

Brian S. Rosner, "Acts and Biblical History" in Bruce W. Winter and Andrew D. Clarke, eds., *The Book of Acts in Its Literary Setting* (Grand Rapids, MI: Eerdmans, 1993), pp. 65–83.

John Van Seters, *In Search of History* (New Haven, CT: Yale University Press, 1983).

For Further Study

Sample some Herodotus or Josephus. To what extent is their style of composition similar to biblical historiography?

BIBLIOGRAPHY

Attridge, Harold W., "Historiography" in *Jewish Writings of the Second Temple Period,* Michael E. Stone, ed. (Philadelphia: Fortress Press, 1984), pp. 157–184.

Baukham, Richard, "Kerygmatic Summaries in the Speeches of Acts" in *History, Literature, and Society in the Book of Acts,* Ben Witherington III, ed. (Cambridge: Cambridge University Press, 1996), pp. 185–217.

Brown, R. E., and John Meier, *Antioch and Rome: New Testament Cradles of Catholic Christianity* (Mahwah, NJ: Paulist Press, 1983).

Brown, Schuyler, *The Origins of Christianity: A Historical Introduction to the New Testament* (Oxford/New York: Oxford University Press, 1984).

Cahill, Michael, "Bible Reading and Genre Recognition," *The Bible Today* (January 1999), 40–44.

Cohen, Shaye, *From the Maccabees to the Mishnah* (Philadelphia: Fortress Press, 1987).

Coote, Robert B., and Mary P. Coote, *Power, Politics, and the Making of the Bible* (Minneapolis: Fortress Press, 1990).

Cross, Frank Moore, *Canaanite Myth and Hebrew Epic* (Cambridge, MA: Harvard University Press, 1973).

Cwiekowski, Frederick J., *The Beginnings of Christianity* (Mahwah, NJ: Paulist Press, 1988).

Dearman, J. Andrew, *Religion and Culture in Ancient Israel* (Peabody, MA: Hendrickson, 1992).

Dever, William G, *What Did the Biblical Writers Know and When Did They Know It?* (Grand Rapids, MI.: Eerdmans, 2001).

Dougherty, Charles T., "Did Paul Fall off a Horse?" *Bible Review* XIII (August 1997), 42–44.

Duggan, Michael, *The Consuming Fire* (San Francisco: Ignatius Press, 1999).

Hemer, Colin, *The Book of Acts in the Setting of Hellenistic History* (Winona Lake, IN: Eisenbrauns, 1990), Chapter 3, "Ancient Historiography."

Kee, Howard Clark, *To Every Nation under Heaven: The Acts of the Apostles* (Harrisburg, PA: Trinity Press, 1997).

Levine, Lee I., "The Age of Hellenism: Alexander the Great and the Rise and Fall of the Hasmonean Kingdom" in *Ancient Israel,* rev. and exp. ed., Herschel Shanks, ed. (Upper Saddle River, NJ: Prentice Hall/Biblical Archaeology Society, 1999), pp. 231–264.

Marguerat, Daniel, "Saul's Conversion (Acts 9, 22, 26) and the Multiplication of Narrative in Acts" in *Luke's Literary Achievement,* C.M. Tuckett, ed. (Sheffield, England: Sheffield Academic Press, 1995), pp. 127–155.

Mason, Steve, *Josephus and the New Testament* (Peabody, MA: Hendrickson, 1992).

McEleney, Neil J., "1–2 Maccabees" in *The New Jerome Biblical Commentary,* pp. 421–425.

Nickelsburg, George W. E., "1 and 2 Maccabees: Same Story, Different Meaning," *Concordia Theological Monthly* 42 (1971), 515–526.

Osiek, Carolyn, "Characters: The Spice of the Story," *The Bible Today* (September 1999), 276–280.

Powell, Mark Allan, *What Are They Saying about Acts?* (Mahwah, NJ: Paulist Press, 1991).

Rosner, Brian S., "Acts and Biblical History" in *The Book of Acts in Its Literary Setting,* Bruce W. Winter and Andrew D. Clarke, eds. (Grand Rapids, MI: Eerdmans, 1993), pp. 65–83.

Shanks, Hershel, ed., *Ancient Israel: From Abraham to the Roman Destruction of the Temple* (Upper Saddle River, NJ: Prentice Hall/Biblical Archaeology Society, 1999).

————, *Christianity and Rabbinic Judaism: A Parallel History of Their Origins and Early Development* (Washington, D.C.: Biblical Archaeology Society, 1992).

Smith, Morton, *Palestinian Parties and Politics That Shaped the Old Testament,* second, corrected ed. (London: SCM Press, 1987).

Spina, Frank Antony, "Reversal of Fortune," *Bible Review* XVII/4 (August 2001), 24–30, 53–54.

Stone, Michael, *Scriptures, Sects, and Visions* (Philadelphia: Fortress Press, 1980).

Taylor, J. Glen, "Was Yahweh Worshiped as the Sun?" *Biblical Archaeology Review* 24/4 (May/June 1994), 52–61, 90–91.

Trible, Phyllis, *Texts of Terror* (Philadelphia: Fortress Press, 1984).

Van Seters, John, *In Search of History* (New Haven, CT: Yale University Press, 1983).

Weinfeld, Moshe, "Deuteronomy's Theological Revolution," *Bible Review* XII/1 (February 1996), 38–41, 44–45.

Wilson, Stephen G., *Related Strangers: Jews and Christians 70–170 C.E.* (Minneapolis: Fortress Press, 1995).

Also Recommended:

1. *Biblical Archaeology Review,* a magazine written by scholars for the general public. See especially the following:

"David's Jerusalem: Fiction or Reality?"—a set of three articles with different conclusions in *Biblical Archaeology Review* 24/4 (July/August 1998).

"The Search for History in the Bible"—a set of three articles in *Biblical Archaeology Review* 26/2 (March/April 2000).

2. *Bible Review,* sister magazine to *BAR,* containing articles relating to texts and interpretation.

INDEX